CYMRU DAFYDD AP GWILYM

DAFYDD AP GWILYM'S WALES

'Nid oes dwyn na dwys dyno
Yn neutu glyn Nant-y-glo
Nis medrwyf o'm nwyf a'm nydd
Heb y llyfr.'

'There's no hill or deep hollow
on either side of Glyn Nant-y-glo
that I do not know, from my passion and pain,
by heart.'

Cymru Dafydd ap Gwilym
Dafydd ap Gwilym's Wales

Cerddi a Lleoedd
Poems and Places

EDITED AND TRANSLATED BY
JOHN K BOLLARD

PHOTOGRAPHS BY
ANTHONY GRIFFITHS

First edition: 2019

ISBN: 978-1-84527-719-2

Cover and book design: Eleri Owen

The publisher acknowledges the financial support of the Welsh Books Council.

Published by Gwasg Carreg Gwalch,
12 Iard yr Orsaf, Llanrwst, Dyffryn Conwy, Cymru LL26 0EH.
tel: 01492 642031
email: llanrwst@carreg-gwalch.cymru
website: www.carreg-gwalch.cymru

Photo of Llawysgrif Hendregadredd, fol. 120, by permission of Llyfrgell
Genedlaethol Cymru / National Library of Wales

Cover photo by Anthony Griffiths: Cwm-y-glo

I Margaret a Marjorie

Cynnwys ✧ Contents

Enfys uwch moryd Dyfi ✧ *Rainbow over the Dyfi estuary*

Rhagair ✧ Preface

Fel un a dreuliodd ei yrfa academaidd yn gweithio ar farddoniaeth Dafydd ap Gwilym, peth amheuthun iawn i mi yw cael golwg newydd ar y pwnc, ond rhaid cyfaddef fod y gyfrol hon wedi agor fy llygaid a pheri i mi weld y cerddi o'r newydd. Mae'r bartneriaeth rhwng John Bollard ac Anthony Griffiths eisoes wedi goleuo nifer o glasuron llenyddol Cymru'r Oesoedd Canol, ac rwy'n hynod o falch bod Dafydd ap Gwilym wedi cael ei le yn y gyfres hon gan fod yr ymdriniaeth ddarluniadol yn gweddu'n neilltuol o dda i'w farddoniaeth ac yn fodd i gyfoethogi ein canfyddiad o'r lleoedd amrywiol ynddi.

Arfera'r ysgolheigion ein rhybuddio mai lleoedd delfrydol y dychymyg llenyddol a ddarlunnir mewn llenyddiaeth ganoloesol, ond eto mae daearyddiaeth Cymru'n ganolog i lawer o waith Dafydd ap Gwilym a'i henwau lleoedd yn britho'i gerddi. Yn eglwys Llanbadarn y mae ei ysbryd yn cyniwair yn anad unlle arall efallai, ond hyd yn oed yn achos cerddi fel 'Trafferth mewn Tafarn' nad ydynt yn enwi lle penodol, anodd yw osgoi lleoli dychmygol yn un o drefi Cymru. A gall unrhyw hen furddun ar fryniau ein gwlad ddwyn i gof yr hiraeth am wynfyd y gorffennol a fynegir mor fyw yn 'Yr Adfail'.

Thema fawr yng ngherddi Dafydd yw'r berthynas agos ond amwys rhwng dyn a byd natur, a natur weithiau'n fendithiol i gariad dynol a thro arall yn rhwystr iddo. Dyma thema sydd wedi dod yn fwy ystyrlon yn sgil pryderon ein hoes ni am ddyfodol yr amgylchedd. Mae ffotograffau hudolus y gyfrol hon yn cynnig cip ar y golygfeydd a welai Dafydd, a hefyd yn ein hatgoffa am barhad bregus tirweddau ein gwlad dros y canrifoedd.

Braf hefyd yw estyn croeso i'r cyfieithiadau newydd yn y gyfrol hon. Gan fod rhaid i bob cyfieithiad llenyddol ddethol elfennau o'r testun gwreiddiol a hepgor eraill – yn enwedig yn achos cerddi mor amlweddog â'r rhain – mae wastad lle i fersiynau sy'n amlygu agweddau newydd.

As one who has spent his academic career working on the poetry of Dafydd ap Gwilym, it is a rare pleasure for me to come across an entirely new way of looking at the subject, but I must say that this book has indeed made me see the poems with fresh eyes. The partnership between John Bollard and Anthony Griffiths has already presented several of the classics of medieval Welsh literature in a new light, and I am delighted that Dafydd ap Gwilym has now been given his place in this series since the illustrative treatment is particularly well suited to his poetry and enriches our perception of the various places depicted in it.

We are often warned by scholars that the places seen in medieval literature are idealized literary topoi, but nevertheless the geography of Wales is central to much of Dafydd ap Gwilym's work and his poems abound in place-names. Llanbadarn church is perhaps the place where his spirit is to be most frequently encountered, but even in the case of poems which do not name any specific place such as 'Trouble at an Inn', it is hard not to imagine a location in one of the towns of Wales. And any of the many ruined buildings on the hillsides of our country can bring to mind the sense of longing for transient joys which is expressed so vividly in 'The Ruin'.

Dafydd ap Gwilym depicts mankind in a close and yet equivocal relationship with the natural world, nature being sometimes beneficent towards human lovemaking and at other times a hindrance to it. This relationship is an aspect of the poetry which has become more meaningful as a result of the concerns of our own age about the future of the natural environment. The marvellous photographs in this volume offer glimpses of the scenes which Dafydd would have known, and also serve as a reminder of the fragile continuity of our country's landscapes over the centuries.

The new translations are another very welcome feature of this book. Since every literary translation must select certain elements of the original text and omit others – especially in the case of such multifaceted poems as these – it is always good to

Rhwng popeth, felly, mae'r casgliad hwn yn gyflwyniad rhagorol i waith Dafydd ap Gwilym.

Dafydd Johnston, Cyfarwyddwr
Canolfan Uwchefrydiau Cymraeg a Cheltaidd

have versions which bring new aspects to the fore. All in all, then, this collection provides a splendid introduction to the poetry of Dafydd ap Gwilym.

Dafydd Johnston, Director
Centre for Advanced Welsh and Celtic Studies

Rhagymadrodd ✧ Introduction

Fe ddisgrifiodd y prydydd Madog Benfras ei gyfaill Dafydd ap Gwilym fel 'paun cerdd' ac 'eos Dyfed', ac fe'i galwyd gan Gruffudd Gryg, cyfaill arall iddo, yn 'benceirddwalch' a 'phaun Dyfed'. O'r bedwaredd ganrif ar ddeg hyd heddiw mae Dafydd wedi cael ei gydnabod fel y gorau o feirdd Cymru. Drwy'r degawdau diweddar, wrth i ymchwilwyr ddarganfod gwybodaeth newydd am ei fywyd a'i noddwyr, a'r merched yr oedd ef yn eu caru, mae ei fri a'i glod wedi tyfu fel un o'r beirdd Ewropeaidd gorau yn yr Oesoedd Canol. Ychwanega'r llyfr hwn ddimensiwn newydd i'r darllenydd â diddordeb ym marddoniaeth Dafydd, ei fywyd a'i yrfa, a'r Gymru yr oedd ef yn byw ynddi. Detholiad sydd yma o gerddi Dafydd yng nghyd-destun y tirlun yr oedd ef yn byw a charu ynddo ac yn teithio drwyddo. Rhydd y ffotograffau gan Anthony Griffiths, ynghyd â'r testunau, y cyfieithiadau, a'r nodiadau, gyfle a dirnadaeth newydd i'r darllenydd cyffredin o farddoniaeth Dafydd sydd yn fwy darluniadol a lliwgar, ac yn caniatáu dealltwriaeth fwy cyflawn na chyfieithiadau ar eu pen eu hunain.

Tra mae ei gerddi yn dangos inni galon Dafydd a'i feddwl, mae ffotograffau Anthony Griffiths yn dangos inni harddwch y byd ffisegol a'r lleoliad daearyddol lle'r oedd Dafydd yn canu i'w gariadon a'i noddwyr a'i gyfeillion. Unwaith eto, mae Anthony wedi teithio ledled y wlad i ddod o hyd i leoedd na fu neb yno ers blynyddoedd, yn aml mewn cors laith yn llawn drysi a rhedyn. Er enghraifft, mewn lle o'r fath y darganfu ef olion o hen dŷ a all fod, o bosibl, yn Gwernyclepa, llys Ifor Hael. Yn eglwys fach Llanrhychwyn, lle y gweddïodd Llywelyn Fawr yn y drydedd ganrif ar ddeg, y tynnodd Anthony lun o ffenestr liw y Drindod – ond yn gyntaf yr oedd yn rhaid iddo ysgubo'r gwe pryf copyn i ffwrdd gyda ffon. Mae ei olygfeydd o'r tirwedd yn ein hatgoffa nid yn unig o harddwch y wlad, ond hefyd o'r ffaith mai dyma'r un Gymru y bu Dafydd yn byw ynddi ac yn ei charu. Ac mae

Dafydd ap Gwilym's friend, the poet Madog Benfras, calls him paun cerdd 'the peacock of poetry' and eos Dyfed 'the nightingale of Dyfed'. Another, Gruffudd Gryg, similarly names him paun Dyfed 'the peacock of Dyfed' and penceirddwalch 'the hawk (i.e, the best) of the chief poets'. From the fourteenth century till now Dafydd ap Gwilym has been recognized throughout Wales as the greatest of early Welsh poets. In recent decades Dafydd's reputation as one of the finest European poets of the Middle Ages has spread considerably further afield as new information about his life, his career, his patrons, and the women he loved has been uncovered by diligent researchers and as new editions and translations of his work have become more widely available. This book adds a new dimension for the interested reader, presenting Dafydd's poetry in the context of the landscape within which he lived, loved, and wandered, giving readers a new lens through which to see the poet and read his poems. This visual accompaniment, along with the texts, translations, and explanatory notes, allows for a more nuanced understanding of and engagement with these poems than would translations alone.

While the poems reveal Dafydd's mind and heart to us, Anthony Griffiths' photographs present the physical and geographic setting of Dafydd's work in striking and beautiful form. In addition to revealing familiar sites and scenes in a new light, Griffiths has travelled to and ferreted out places whose locations have been all but forgotten or hidden in brambles and bracken where no one else thought (or had the tenacity) to look, and he has photographed them with skill and artistry. Lesser-known places and artifacts, for example, include the possible remains of Gwernyclepa, the house of Ifor Hael, Dafydd's beloved patron, as well as the stained-glass nun and the carved rood beam with its allegorical representation of redemption and resurrection, both from Llanllugan. Anthony's striking views of the Welsh landscape as it is today serve to remind us not only of the beauty of Wales, but also that in many ways this is the

12

barddoniaeth Dafydd yn ein dysgu i werthfawrogi ei mynyddoedd a'i hafonydd, ei bryniau a'i dyffrynnoedd, ei gwŷdd ac adar, boed yn yr haf gogoneddus neu'r gaeaf rhewllyd. Ar ôl bron i saith can mlynedd, mae'n resynus ond ddim yn syndod, fod llawer o'r cestyll a'r tai lle bu Dafydd yn aros ynddynt bellach yn adfeilion. Mae'r byd naturiol a garai Dafydd wedi gweld newid mawr hefyd, er y byddai ef yn parhau i adnabod llawer ohono. Efallai y bydd y ffotograffau a'r cerddi hyn i gyd yn ein helpu ninnau i feddwl am y gorffennol, wrth gwrs, ond hefyd am y presennol a'r dyfodol ac am ein lle ni ym myd Dafydd heddiw.

Er mwyn taflu goleuni ar deithiau Dafydd a'i ddylanwad fel bardd yng Nghymru, dewiswyd cerddi lle mae Dafydd yn enwi lleoedd a phersonau yn benodol ac ymhlyg. Mae rhai o'r cerddi wedi eu dewis hefyd i ddangos ystod diddordebau Dafydd – ei ganu serch, ei ganu moliant, ac wrth gwrs, ei *persona* fel tipyn o ddigrifwas sy'n glaf o gariad. Ac rydym wedi ceisio cynrychioli gwahanol ffurfiau o'i gerddi – cywyddau, gan mwyaf, ond awdl ac englyn hefyd. Mae Dafydd yn fardd comig gwych, yn ein hannog i chwerthin ar ei ben ac felly i ddysgu chwerthin am ein pennau ein hunain ac efallai deall ein hunain yn well. Mae'n ein dysgu ni sut i garu, a sut i garu'n anghymwys, a sut i barhau'n obeithiol pan fydd cariad yn ymddangos yn anobeithiol. Hynod yw cerddi Dafydd i'w noddwyr am y cyfuniad agos o'i gyfeillgarwch dilys, calonnog, a'i ddiolchgarwch dwfn iddynt hwy fel bardd. Ac er nad ydym yn meddwl amdano fel bardd crefyddol, y mae cerddi crefyddol Dafydd yn argyhoeddiadol a chynhyrfus. Hyd yn oed mewn cerdd ddigrif fel *Trafferth mewn Tafarn*, mae hi'n bosibl synhwyro ei ffydd. Yn wir, mae'r gerdd honno yn ein rhybuddio i osgoi ymddygiad pechadurus o'r fath (er gwaethaf ddadleuon Dafydd yn *Y Bardd a'r Brawd Llwyd*).

Nid crefft ysgrifenedig oedd barddoniaeth Gymraeg yn yr Oesoedd Canol. Cyfansoddwyd cerddi ar lafar i'w hadrodd neu eu canu i gyfeiliant telyn gan y bardd o flaen cynulleidfa. Byddent ar gof y bardd a beirdd eraill ac yn

same Wales that Dafydd knew, loved, and still today teaches us to appreciate more fully – its mountains and rivers, hills and valleys, trees and birds, whether in glorious summer or icy winter. After more than 600 years it is lamentable but not surprising that many of the places Dafydd knew and loved lie in ruins. Even the natural world in which he took such delight has seen great change, though he would undoubtedly still recognize much. Thus, these photos may help us to ponder not just the country's past, but its present, its future, and our place in it as well.

In order to illuminate the extent of Dafydd's travels and his influence as a poet throughout Wales, the selection of poems has been guided in great measure by places which Dafydd names, either explicitly or implicitly. Poems have also been chosen to reflect Dafydd's range of interests, his expressions of love, praise of his patrons, and self-satire, as well as his command of different themes, moods, and verse forms. We have tried to represent Dafydd in his wonderful variety. He is a superbly comic poet, encouraging us to laugh at him and thereby learn not only to laugh at ourselves, but to understand ourselves better. He also teaches us how to love, how not to love, and to continue to hope even when love itself seems hopeless. Dafydd's poems to his patrons are remarkable for their combination of his heartfelt and deep friendship inextricably intertwined with his gratitude to them as a poet. And though Dafydd is not generally thought of as a religious poet, even in his most comic verse, such as Trafferth mewn Tafarn 'Trouble at an Inn', his faith is audible, and his explicitly religious poetry is as moving – and convincing – as any.

Poetry in medieval Wales was not a written art. Poems were composed orally and sung or recited to audiences, often to the accompaniment of a harp. They were remembered and passed on by the poets themselves, by other poets, and by professional datgeiniaid, reciters whose function was to perform a poem on demand, yn gwbl megis y cano y prydydd 'exactly as the poet would sing it', as the contemporary poetic grammars put it. It may be that other early manuscripts have been lost, but, aside from three poems copied onto blank pages in two

arbennig datgeiniaid. Swydd y datgeiniad oedd cyflwyno cerdd 'yn gwbl megis y canodd y prydydd', fel y dywed *Gramadegau'r Penceirddiaid* o'r bedwaredd ganrif ar ddeg (GP 17). Diamau fod llawer o lawysgrifau cynnar wedi mynd ar goll; sut bynnag does dim ond tair cerdd a gopiwyd ar dudalennau gwag, efallai yn ystod bywyd Dafydd, wedi goroesi i ni. Fe ddarganfyddir y rhan fwyaf o'i gerddi mewn llawysgrifau a gyfansoddwyd ganrif a mwy ar ôl ei farwolaeth. Yn anffodus, ni wyddom yn union pryd y bu Dafydd farw. Oddeutu 1350 neu 1370 yw'r amcandybiau gorau. Heb gronoleg awdurdodol i Ddafydd na'i gerddi ychwaith, rydym wedi dosbarthu'r cerddi yn y llyfr hwn dan y penawdau **Morfudd, Dyddgu, Merched heb eu Henwi, Noddwyr a Beirdd**, ac **'ac ni chanaf mwy'**. Y mae'r bennod olaf yn dipyn o fyfyrdod ar fywyd Dafydd a'i gladdedigaeth.

Nid barddoniaeth ('poetry' *per se*) yw'r cyfieithiadau sydd yma. Ceisiais gyfieithu synnwyr y Gymraeg mor agos ag y gallwn, heb boeni'n ormodol am sŵn y Saesneg. Ond pe bai, o bryd i'w gilydd, rhyw odl, atsain, neu gyflythreniad yn dod yn naturiol, ni wrthwynebais – cyhyd â'i fod yn gymorth i'r bwriad a'r effaith gwreiddiol. Gyda'r testunau Cymraeg, beth bynnag, yr wyf yn ymwybodol o *dictum* Twm Morys: 'Gwell yw sŵn heb synnwyr na synnwyr heb sŵn.' Dyna nerth y gynghanedd. Mae sylwadau byr ar gynghanedd a mydr yn 'Brief Introduction to Welsh Metrics.'

Fe gyhoeddwyd *Gwaith Dafydd ap Gwilym* gan Thomas Parry yn 1952. Hwn oedd y golygiad cyntaf i sefydlu'r canon, o'r rhan fwyaf, o waith Dafydd. Ers hynny, mae llawer o ymchwil gofalus wedi cael ei wneud ar gerddi unigol ac ar fyd Dafydd a'i gyfoeswyr. Yn 2007 fe gyhoeddodd Dafydd Johnston a thîm o ysgolheigion safle Gwe bwysig, dafyddapgwilym.net (o hyn ymlaen DG.net), gyda golygiadau newydd o holl gerddi Dafydd, gan gynnwys rhai nad oeddynt yng ngolygiad Parry. Yn 2010 fe ymddangosodd fersiwn printiedig o *Cerddi Dafydd ap Gwilym*. Heb y gweithiau hyn ni fyddai'r llyfr hwn yn bosibl. Yr ydym yn ddiolchgar iawn i'r Athro Johnston a'i

manuscripts, copies of Dafydd's poetry do not begin to appear until about 100 or 150 years after Dafydd's death. And, unfortunately, we do not even know with any specificity when he died. The best estimates range from c. 1350 to c. 1370. Without a reliable chronology for either the poet or his poems, we have grouped the poems in this book according to whom or for whom he sang them: **Morfudd, Dyddgu, Unnamed Girls, Patrons and Poets**, and finally *'and I shall sing no more'*, a brief meditation, as it were, on Dafydd's life and his burial.

Rather than try to render these poems into English verse, I have recast in prose as clearly as possible what I perceive to be the meaning of the original and to replicate the order and structure of Dafydd's phrasing as closely as is compatible with clarity. That said, occasionally there have been times when some assonance or alliteration has presented itself and I have not resisted – as long as I thought it helped to convey the intent and the effect of the original. To those who do not read or understand Welsh, I encourage you to take some time to look at and perhaps puzzle over the Welsh text, even if it is just a line or two now and then. The rhymes within and at the end of lines and the matching and repeated consonants which comprise the cynghanedd, the harmony of the verse, will become visible if you look carefully. It is often remarked that the sound of Welsh poetry in the strict metres, as these poems are, is as important as the meaning of the words. That is true, of course, of poetry in any language, but it is no exaggeration to say that in Welsh the relationship between sound and sense is extraordinarily intimate and detailed. Some hints and guidelines for exploring the inextricability of the two are given in the 'Brief Introduction to Welsh Metrics.'

Much research has been done since the appearance of Thomas Parry's magisterial Gwaith Dafydd ap Gwilym (1952, 1963), and the entire canon of Dafydd's work has been revaluated, revised, and reedited by Dafydd Johnston and others and published as Cerddi Dafydd ap Gwilym (2010) and online at dafyddapgwilym.net (2007, hereafter DG.net). Without their painstaking work this book would hardly have been possible. We are immensely grateful to Professor Johnston

gydweithwyr am eu caniatâd i adargraffu'r testunau Cymraeg yma. Ni allaf ond gobeithio imi wneud cyfiawnder a hwy, hyd yn oed lle gall ein dehongliadau fod yn wahanol. Mae cyfieithiadau Saesneg o'r cyfan neu llawer o farddoniaeth Dafydd wedi'u cyhoeddi gan Richard Loomis (1982), Rachel Bromwich (1982), Gwyn Thomas (2001), DG.net (2007), a Joseph Clancy (2016). Ein gobaith yw fod cynnwys y testunau Cymraeg yn y gyfrol hon yn fanteisiol a defnyddiol i siaradwyr Cymraeg ac y bydd darllenwyr di-Gymraeg yn cael cipolwg ynddynt ar gymhlethdod a gwychder y cerddi yn yr hen iaith. Fe ddylai barddoniaeth y meistri, mewn unrhyw iaith, gael ei gyfieithu mor aml â phosibl i roi i eraill syniad o'r meddylfryd a'r weledigaeth a geir mewn diwylliannau gwahanol. Mae hyn yn arbennig a mwyfwy pwysig i ieithoedd lleiafrifol, yn yr oes ddigidol hon, gyda'r gwastatu diwyllianol sy'n digwydd yn ddyddiol.

and his colleagues for permission to reproduce their edited Welsh texts. I can only hope that I have done them justice, even when our interpretations might differ. Translations of all or much of Dafydd's poetry have been published by Richard Loomis (1982), Rachel Bromwich (1982), Gwyn Thomas (2001), DG.net (2007), and most recently Joseph Clancy (2016). We hope that the inclusion of the Welsh texts will make this book attractive and useful to Welsh speaking readers and provide for non-Welsh speakers a window into the intricacies and beauties of Welsh verse. Great poetry deserves to be translated as frequently as possible into other languages in order to give those who are not familiar with the original texts a variety of insights into the artistry, the minds, and the unique cultural perspectives of the poets who represent, in ways that others cannot, the people amongst whom they live or lived. This is doubly important in the case of so-called minority languages and cultures, especially in the face of the profound cultural leveling taking place in this electronic and digitized age.

Acknowledgements

Our profound thanks are due to John and Linda Howdle, Dafydd Johnston, Steve Kilby, David Lloyd, Brynley Lloyd-Bollard, Catrin Lloyd-Bollard, Rheinallt Llwyd, Henry Lyman, Nicola Morgan, William Oram, Helen Parker, James Riddle, David & Chris Rose, and many other friends and colleagues who have listened patiently, provided both excellent advice and much-appreciated encouragement, and granted access to their property. To express thanks adequately to Margaret Lloyd and Marjorie Griffiths, our wives and companions, would require a poet as eloquent as Dafydd ap Gwilym himself. They have supported us, cheered us on, and accompanied us every step, indeed every inch, of the way. And they have been eagle-eyed editors and shrewd critics who have corrected our mistakes both large and small. The responsibility for any mistakes that remain is entirely our own. Many thanks, too, to all at Gwasg Carreg Gwalch, especially Mererid Jones and Eleri Owen. And stepping out of the editorial plural, it pleases me to say that Anthony Griffiths has once more outdone himself in this, our fifth collaboration. The first fifty years of our friendship have been a great pleasure. Here's to the future.

Edrych ar draws y Fenai i Drwyn Abermenai ✧ *Looking across the Menai to Abermenai Point*

Afon Llyfni yn llifo i'r môr ✧ *The Llyfni entering the sea*

Pererindod Merch

Gwawr ddyhuddiant y cantref,
Lleian aeth er llu o nef
Ac er Non, calon a'i cêl,
Ac er Dewi, Eigr dawel,
O Fôn deg, poed rhwydd, rhegddi
I Fynyw dir, f'enaid i,
I geisio, blodeuo'r blaid,
Maddeuaint, am a ddywaid,
Am ladd ei gwas dulas dig,
Penydiwr cul poenedig.
O alanas gwas gwawdferw
Yr aeth, oer hiraeth, ar herw.

Greddf fföes gruddiau ffion.
Gadewis fy newis Fôn.
Crist Arglwydd, boed rhwydd, bid trai,
Gas, a chymwynas, Menai.
Llifnant, geirw luddiant guraw,
Llyfni, bo hawdd drwyddi draw.
Y Traeth Mawr, cludfawr air clod,
Treia, gad fyned trwod.
Y Bychan Draeth, gaeth gerrynt,
Gad i'm dyn gwyn hyn o hynt.
Darfu'r gweddïau dirfawr:
Digyffro fo Ertro fawr.
Talwn fferm porth Abermaw
Ar don drai er ei dwyn draw.
Gydne gwin, gad, naw gwaneg
Dysynni, i dir Dewi deg.
A dwfn yw tonnau Dyfi,
Dŵr rhyn, yn ei herbyn hi.
Rheidol, gad er d'anrhydedd
Heol i fun hael o fedd.

A Girl's Pilgrimage

The cantref's lady of reconciliation,
a maiden, went for the sake of the heavenly host
and for Non – heart hides it –
4 and for Dewi – a quiet Eigr –
from fair Môn – may she be free –
towards the land of Mynyw – my dear one
to seek – may her party prosper –
8 forgiveness for what she said,
for slaying her bruised and sorrowful lad,
a thin, pained penitent.
For the murder of a lad bubbling with praise
12 she went – cold longing – into exile.

The rosy-cheeked one hurried off.
My chosen one left Môn.
Lord Christ, easy and at ebb
16 may the harsh but kindly Menai remain.
The rushing stream – pounding barrier of foam –
of the Llyfni, may it be easy to pass through.
Y Traeth Mawr – widespread its fame –
20 recede! Let her go through.
Y Traeth Bychan – narrow course –
let my fair girl go this way.
The extensive prayers are over.
24 May the great Artro be calm.
I would pay the toll at Barmouth harbour
for carrying her across on ebbing waves.
Allow the wine-colored one, nine waves
28 of Dysynni, to go to fair Dewi's land.
And deep are the Dyfi waves,
rough water, facing her.
Rheidol, allow, for the sake of your honour,
32 passage to a maiden generous with mead.

Y Traeth Mawr ac Eryri ✧ *Y Traeth Mawr and the Snowdon Range*

Afon Dysynni, gyda Chadair Idris a Chraig Aderyn ✧ *The Dysynni, with Cadair Idris and Craig Aderyn*

Ystwyth, ym mhwyth, gad ym hon,
Dreistew ddwfr, dros dy ddwyfron.
Aeron, ferw hyson hoywserch,
Gad trwod fyfyrglod ferch.
Teifi deg, tyfiad eigiawn,
Gad i'r dyn gadeirio'r dawn.
Durfing drwy'r afon derfyn
Yr êl ac y dêl y dyn.

Ystwyth, as a reward, allow her for me,
deep fierce water, over your breast.
Aeron, bubbling and loud like a lively lover,
allow through you a renowned, thoughtful maid.
Fair Teifi, filler of the deep,
allow the girl to increase her virtue.
Fervently over the river's edge
may the girl come and go.

'Y Bychan Draeth – gaeth gerrynt' ✧ *'Y Traeth Bychan – narrow course'*

Mau hirffawd, mae ym mhorffor,
Os byw, rhwng Mynyw a môr.
Os hi a'm lladdodd, oes hir,
Herw hylithr, hwyr yr holir.
Maddeuaint Mair, neddair nawdd,
I'm lleddf wylan a'm lladdawdd.
Diau, a mi a'i diaur,
Minnau a'i maddau i'm aur.

Great fortune is mine – she is in purple –
if I live – between Mynyw and the sea.
If she has slain me – a long time –
44 *elusive in exile, she will be tried at last.*
Mary's forgiveness, and her protective hand,
for my gentle seagull who slew me.
Without doubt – and I shall acquit her –
48 *I shall forgive my golden one.*

Eglwys Gadeiriol Tyddewi, Mynyw ✧ St David's Cathedral, Mynyw

Morfudd

'Bedwlwyn o'r coed mwyn' ✧ *'The birch grove in the gentle wood'*

Offeren y Llwyn

Lle digrif y bûm heddiw
Dan fentyll y gwyrddgyll gwiw,
Yn gwarando ddechrau dydd
Y ceiliog bronfraith celfydd
Yn canu ynglyn alathr,
Arwyddion a llithion llathr.

Pellennig, Pwyll ei annwyd,
Pell siwrneiai'r llatai llwyd.
Yma doeth o swydd goeth Gaer
Am ei erchi o'm eurchwaer,
Geiriog, hyd pan geir gwarant,
Sef y cyrch, yn entyrch nant.
Amdano yr oedd gamsai
O flodau mwyn geinciau Mai,
A'i gasul, dybygesynt,
O esgyll, gwyrdd fentyll, gwynt.
Nid oedd yna, myn Duw mawr,
Ond aur oll yn do'r allawr.
Morfudd a'i hanfonasai
Mydr ganiadaeth mab maeth Mai.

The Mass of the Grove

I was in a pleasant place today
under mantles of fine green hazel
listening at the break of day
4 to the skilful speckle-breasted thrush
singing a polished englyn,
sacred signs and polished lessons.

Far-traveller, with Pwyll's nature,
8 far the grey-brown messenger journeyed.
He came here from the fine district of Carmarthen
because my golden girl asked him,
eloquent one, until a pledge is obtained.
12 He made for the head of the valley.
About him was an alb
of the flowers on the tender May branches,
and his chasuble, they would have supposed,
16 of wings, green mantles, wind.
There was nothing, by great God,
but pure gold as a roof over the altar.
Morfudd had sent it,
20 the metered singing of the foster son of May.

Mi a glywwn mewn gloywiaith
Ddatganu, nid methu, maith,
Ddarllain i'r plwyf, nid rhwyf rhus,
Efengyl yn ddifyngus.
Codi ar fryn ynn yna
Afrlladen o ddeilien dda,
Ac eos gain fain fangaw
O gwr y llwyn ger ei llaw,
Clerwraig nant, i gant a gân
Cloch aberth, clau a chwiban,
A dyrchafael yr aberth
Hyd y nen uwchben y berth,
A chrefydd i'n Dofydd Dad
 charegl nwyf a chariad.
Bodlon wyf i'r ganiadaeth,
Bedwlwyn o'r coed mwyn a'i maeth.

I heard in a clear voice
chanting, not ceasing, long-lasting,
reading to the parish, no pompous hesitation,
24   *the gospel without mumbling,*
raising on a hill of ash-trees there
a blessed leaf as the eucharistic host,
and the beautiful, high-pitched, eloquent nightingale
28   *from the corner of the grove nearby,*
wandering poetess of the valley, rings for a hundred
the sanctus bell, loud the trill,
and he elevates the host
32   *up to the heavens above the grove,*
and devotion to our Lord God the Father
with a chalice of desire and love.
I am pleased with the singing.
36   *The birch grove in the gentle wood fosters it.*

Y Fun o Eithinfynydd

Y fun o Eithinfynydd,
F'enaid teg, ni fyn oed dydd.
Feinion aeliau, fwyn olwg,
Fanwallt aur, fuanwyllt wg,
Fy ngwynfyd rhag trymfryd tranc,
Fy nuwies addwyn ieuanc,
Fy nrych, llewych mewn lliwaur,
Fy rhan yw, fy rhiain aur,
Fy swllt dan fynwes elltydd,
Fy serch ar hon fwyfwy sydd.
Fy nillyn mwynwyn manwallt,
Fy nghrair ni chair yn uwch allt.
Ni chyrch hon goed y fron fry,
Ni châr a'i câr, ni chwery.
Ni chair Morfudd i chwarae:
Nych air, caru Mair y mae
A charu'r saint gwych hoywrym
A charu Duw. Ni chred ym.
Ni ŵyr gwen, anoriog wyf,
Nid edwyn mo'r oed ydwyf.
Ni adwaeniad odineb,
Ni fynnai 'nyn fi na neb.
Ni fynnwn innau, f'anwyl,
Fyw oni chawn fun wych wyl.
Am hynny darfu 'mhoeni.
Morfudd fwyn, marw fyddaf fi.

The Girl from Eithinfynydd

The girl from Eithinfynydd,
my fair friend, does not want to meet me.
Slender brows, genteel look,
4   fine golden hair, swift fierce frown,
my paradise to ward off thoughts of death,
my splendid young goddess,
my mirror, radiance in a golden hue,
8   my share is she, my golden girl,
my treasure below the bosom of the hills,
my love for her grows more and more.
My genteel, fair, fine-haired darling,
12   my treasure will not be found on a high slope.
She does not go to the wood up on the hill.
She does not love one who loves her; she does not play.
Morfudd will not be found to play.
16   Painful word: she loves Mary
and loves the splendid mighty saints
and loves God. She does not believe in me.
The fair girl does not know – I am unwavering –
20   she is not aware of the state I am in.
She is not familiar with wantonness;
my dear one did not want me or anyone.
And I would not want – my distress –
24   to live if I could not have the fine modest girl.
Because of that I have suffered pain.
Gentle Morfudd, I shall die!

Aran Benllyn o Eithinfynydd ✧ *Aran Benllyn from Eithinfynydd*

Morfudd fel yr Haul

Gorllwyn ydd wyf ddyn geirllaes,
Gorlliw eiry mân marian maes.
Gwŷl, Dduw, mae golau o ddyn,
Goleuach nog ael ewyn.
Goleudon lafarfron liw,
Goleudaer ddyn, gŵyl ydiw.
Gŵyr obryn serch gerdd o'm pen,
Goreubryd haul ger wybren,
Gwawr y bobl, gwiwra bebyll,
Gŵyr hi gwatwaru gŵr hyll,
Gwiw Forfudd, gwae oferfardd
Gwan a'i câr, Gwenhwyfar hardd.
Gwe aur, llun y dyn, gwae ef
Gwiw ei ddelw yn gwaeddolef.

Mawr yw ei thwyll a'i hystryw,
Mwy no dim, a'm enaid yw.
Y naill wers yr ymddengys
Fy nyn gan rhwng llan a llys,
A'r llall, ddyn falchgall fylchgaer,
Yr ymgudd gloyw Forfudd glaer,
Mal haul ymylau hoywles,
Mamaeth tywysogaeth tes,
Moliannus yw ei syw swydd,
Maeleres Mai oleurwydd,
Mawr ddisgwyl Morfudd ddisglair,
Mygrglaer ddrych mireinwych Mair.

Morfudd like the Sun

I am waiting for a soft-spoken girl,
the brilliance of small snow in a stony field.
See, God, that she is a bright girl,
4 *brighter than a crest of foam,*
the color of the breast of a loud, bright wave.
A fervently bright girl, she is modest.
She knows how to win a love poem from my lips –
8 *the fairest face of the sun near a cloud.*
The people's dawn in a fine fur mantle,
she knows how to mock an ugly man.
Excellent Morfudd! Woe to a feeble lowly poet
12 *who loves her, a beautiful Gwenhwyfar!*
The girl's appearance is a web of gold. Woe to him –
handsome his image – crying out in woe!

Great is her deception and her cunning,
16 *greater than anything, but she is my dear.*
One time my fair girl appears
between church and court,
and another – proud wise girl on the fortress battlements –
20 *bright shining Morfudd hides herself,*
like the sun, beneficial to the land.
Foster-mother of the principality of warmth,
her excellent work is praiseworthy,
24 *May's merchant of radiance,*
the striking appearance of bright Morfudd,
the bright majestic semblance of lovely, magnificent Mary.

Machlud haul y tu ôl i Gastell Aberystwyth ✧ *Sunset behind Aberystwyth Castle*

Hyd y llawr, dirfawr derfyn,
Haul a ddaw mal hyloyw ddyn
Yn deg o fewn corff un dydd,
Bugeiles wybr bwygilydd.
Pan fo, poen fawr a wyddem,
Raid wrth yr haul a draul drem,
Gwedy dêl, prif ryfel praff,
Dros ei phen wybren obraff
Y diainc ymron duaw,
Naws poen ddig, y nos pan ddaw.

Across the earth, enormous territory,
the sun comes like a shining girl,
pleasantly within the compass of a single day –
shepherdess of the sky from one end to the other.
When there is – we have known great pain –
a need for the sun which dazzles the sight,
after a thick cloud – very great conflict –
comes over her face,
she escapes just before dark
– a feeling of sorrowful pain – as night comes.

Dylawn fydd yr wybr dulas,
Delw Eluned, blaned blas.
Pell i neb wybod yna,
Pêl yw i Dduw, pa le'dd â.
Ni chaiff llaw yrthiaw wrthi,
Nac ymafael â'i hael hi.
Trannoeth y dyrchaif hefyd,
Ennyn o bell nen y byd.

Nid annhebig, ddig ddogni,
Ymachludd Morfudd â mi:
Gwedy dêl o'r awyr fry,
Ar hyd wybr y rhed obry,
Yr ymachludd teg ei gwg
Dan orddrws y dyn oerddrwg.

Emlynais nwyf am lannerch
Y Penrhyn, eisyddyn serch.
Peunydd y gwelir yno
Pefrddyn doeth, a pheunoeth ffo.
Nid nes cael ar lawr neuadd
Daro llaw, deryw fy lladd,
Nog fydd, ddyn gwawdrydd gwiwdraul,
I ddwylo rhai ddaly yr haul.
Nid oes rhagorbryd pefrlon
Gan yr haul gynne ar hon.
Os tecaf un eleni,
Tecaf, hil naf, yw'n haul ni.

Paham, eiddungam ddangos,
Na ddeaill y naill y nos,
A'r llall yn des ysblennydd,
Olau da, i liwio dydd?
Bei ymddangosai'r ddeubryd
O gylch i bedwar bylch byd,
Rhyfeddod llyfr dalensyth
Yn oes bun dyfod nos byth.

The blue-black sky will be full,
image of Eluned, the planet's place.
Hard for anyone to know then –
40 *she is God's ball – where she goes.*
No hand can touch her,
nor grasp her edge.
On the morrow she will rise again,
44 *lighting up from afar the roof of the world.*

Not dissimilar – sharing sorrow –
is Morfudd setting from me:
after she comes from the air above,
48 *across the sky she runs below,*
she sets – fair her frown –
under the lintel of the cold, wretched man.

I pursued desire around the region
52 *of Penrhyn, home of love.*
Every day a wise sparkling girl
is seen there, and every night she flees.
I'm no nearer to getting, on the floor of a hall,
56 *to touch her hand – I am slain –*
than it would be – freely praised, dazzling girl –
for people's hands to seize the sun.
The blazing sun has
60 *no better, radiant, happy face than she.*
If one is fairest this year,
fairest – of a lord's lineage – is our sun.

Why – to take a desirable step –
64 *does not the one comprehend the night*
and the other, in splendid warmth,
good light, color the day?
If their two faces appeared
68 *in circuit around the four corners of the earth,*
it would be a wonder in a stiff-leaved book
if, in the maiden's life, night ever came.

Dan y Bargod

Clo a roed ar ddrws y tŷ,
Claf wyf o serch, clyw fyfy.
Dyred i'th weled, wiwlun,
Er Duw hael, aro dy hun.
Geirffug ferch, pam y gorffai?
Gorffwyll, myn Mair, a bair bai.

Taro, o'm annwyd dyrys,
Tair ysbonc, torres y bys
Cloëdig, un clau ydoedd,
A'i clywewch chwi? Sain cloch oedd.
Morfudd, fy nghrair diweirbwyll,
Mamaeth tywysogaeth twyll,
Mau wâl am y wialen
â thi, rhaid ym weiddi, wen.
Tosturia fy anhunglwyf,
Tywyll yw'r nos, twyllwr nwyf.
Adnebydd flined fy nhro,
Wb o'r hin o'r wybr heno!
Aml yw'r rhëydr o'r bargawd,
Ermig nwyf, ar y mau gnawd.

Under the Eaves

The door of the house was locked.
I am sick with love, hear me!
Come to be seen, lovely form.
4   For generous God's sake, wake up!
A false-spoken girl – why should she prevail?
A fault, by Mary, that causes madness.

Striking, because of my great passion,
8   three blows, the locked latch
broke – it was a loud one.
Could you hear it? It was as loud as a bell!
Morfudd, my chaste-natured darling,
12   foster-mother of the principality of treachery,
mine is a shelter on the other side of the wall
from you. I need to shout, fair maid.
Have mercy on my fevered sleeplessness.
16   The night is dark, a traitor to desire.
Acknowledge how miserable my situation is.
Oh! for the weather from the heavens tonight!
The cataracts from the eaves are copious
20   – desire's instrument – on this flesh of mine.

Castell Caernarfon ✧ *Caernarfon Castle*

Nid mwy y glaw, neud mau glwyf,
No'r ôd dano yr ydwyf.
Nid esmwyth hyn o dysmwy,
Ni bu boen ar farwgroen fwy
Nog a gefais drwy ofal,
Ym Gŵr a'm gwnaeth, nid gwaeth gwâl.
Ni bu'n y Gaer yn Arfon
Geol waeth no'r heol hon.
Ni byddwn allan hyd nos,
Ni thechwn ond o'th achos.
Ni ddown i oddef, od gwn,
Beunoeth gur be na'th garwn.
Ni byddwn dan law ac ôd
Ennyd awr onid erod.
Ni faddeuwn, gwn gyni,
Y byd oll oni bai di.

Yma ydd wyf trwy annwyd,
Tau ddawn, yn y tŷ ydd wyd.
Amau fydd gan a'm hirglyw
Yma, fy aur, ymy fyw.
Yna y mae f'enaid glân
A'm ellyll yma allan.
Ymaith fy meddwl nid â,
Amwyll a'm peris yma.
Amod â mi a wneddwyd,
Yma ydd wyf, a mae 'dd wyd?

The rain is no greater – sickness is mine –
than the snow I am under.
This shivering is not comfortable.
24 There was never greater pain on numb skin
than I have got through caring,
by the One who made me, no worse shelter.
There was never in Caernarfon
28 a worse jail than this court-yard.
I would not be out all night,
I would not lurk about but because of you.
Indeed, I would not come to suffer
32 anguish every night if I did not love you.
I would not be in the rain and snow
for the space of an hour if not for you.
I would not forsake – I know affliction –
36 the whole world if it were not for you.

Here I am because of passion.
Your good fortune: you are in the house.
Whoever listens long to me here
40 will doubt, my golden one, that I am alive.
In there is my pure soul
and my soulless self is here outside.
My thoughts will not go away.
44 Madness caused me to be here.
You made a pact with me.
Here I am, and where are you?

Cyrchu Lleian

Dadlitia'r diwyd latai,
Hwnt o'r mars dwg hynt i'r mai.
Gedaist, ciliaist, myn Celi,
Arnaf y mae d'eisiau di.
Dof holion, difai helynt,
Da fuost lle gwyddost gynt.
Peraist ym fun ar ungair,
Pâr ym weled merched Mair.

Making Advances to a Nun

Do not be angry, faithful go-between;
take a journey across the March to the plains.
You left, you departed, by Heaven;
4   *I have need of you.*
Mild requests, faultless voyage,
you did well – you know where – earlier:
you got me a maiden with a single word.
8   *Now get me to see the girls of Mary.*

Llanllugan

Abades Lanllugan ✧
The Abbess of Llanllugan

Dewis lyry, dos i Lan falch
Llugan, lle mae rhai lliwgalch.
Cais yn y llan ac annerch
Y sieler mawr, selwr merch.
Dywaid, glaim diwyd y glêr,
Hon yw'r salm, hyn i'r sieler,
A chŵyn maint yw'r achwyn mau
A chais ym fynachesau.
Saint o bob lle a'm gweheirdd
Santesau hundeiau heirdd,
Gwyn eiry, arial gwawn oror,
Gwenoliaid, cwfeiniaid côr,
Chwiorydd bedydd bob un
I Forfudd, araf eurfun.

O'i caf innau rhag gofal
O'r ffreutur dyn eglur dâl,
Oni ddaw er cludaw clod,
Hoywne eiry, honno erod,
Da ddodrefn yw dy ddeudroed,
Dwg o'r côr ddyn deg i'r coed,
Câr trigain cariad rhagor,
Cais y glochyddes o'r côr,
Cais frad ar yr abades
Cyn lleuad haf, ceinlliw tes,
Un a'i medr, einym adail,
Â'r lliain du, i'r llwyn dail.

Choose your paths. Go to Llan-proud-
Llugan, where there are some lime-white ones.
Ask at the church and greet
12 *the great jailer, girl's guardian.*
Say – the poet's persistent claim,
this is the psalm – this to the jailer,
and complain how great is my complaint,
16 *and seek nuns for me.*
Saints from all over forbid me
the lovely holy women of the dormitory,
snow white, like hillside gossamer,
20 *swallows, a choir of nuns,*
sisters in faith, each one,
to Morfudd, gentle golden girl.

If I can get, to ward off sorrow,
24 *from the refectory a clear-browed girl,*
if that one does not come, despite piling praise on her,
– snow's bright hue – for you
– your feet are good implements –
28 *fetch a fair girl from the choir to the woods,*
sister of sixty more sweethearts.
Try the bellringer from the choir.
Try trickery on the abbess
32 *before the summer moon, fair colour of sunshine,*
one who will come – ours a bower –
with a black habit, to the grove of leaves.

Galw ar Ddwynwen

Dwynwen deigr arien degwch,
Da y gŵyr o gôr fflamgwyr fflwch
Dy ddelw aur diddoluriaw
Digion druain ddynion draw.
Dyn a wylio, gloywdro glân,
Yn dy gôr, Indeg eirian,
Nid oes glefyd na bryd brwyn
A êl ynddo o Landdwyn.

Dy laesblaid yw dy lwysblwyf,
Dolurus ofalus wyf.
Y fron hon o hoed gordderch
Y sydd yn unchwydd o serch,
Hirwayw o sail gofeiliaint,
Herwydd y gwn, hwn yw haint,
Oni chaf, o byddaf byw,
Forfudd, llyna oferfyw.
Gwna fi yn iach, wiwiach wawd,
O'm anwychder a'm nychdawd.
Cymysg lateirwydd flwyddyn
Â rhadau Duw rhod a dyn.
Nid rhaid, ddelw euraid ddilyth,
Yt ofn pechawd fethlgnawd fyth.
Nid adwna, da ei dangnef,
Duw a wnaeth, nid ai o nef.
Ni'th wŷl mursen eleni
Yn hustyng yn yng â ni.
Ni rydd Eiddig ddig ddygnbwyll
War ffon i ti, wyry ei phwyll.
Tyn, o'th obr, taw, ni thybir
Wrthyd, wyry gymhlegyd hir,
O Landdwyn, dir gynired,
I Gwm-y-gro, gem o Gred.

Appealing to St Dwynwen

Dwynwen, fair as frosty tears,
from a choir of bright candles your golden image
knows well how to ease
4 *the sorrows of wretched folk there.*
For anyone who keeps vigil – bright, holy time –
in your choir, fair Indeg,
no sickness nor time of sadness
8 *goes with him from Llanddwyn.*

Your humble flock is your fair parish.
I am sad and troubled.
From longing for a lover this breast
12 *is nigh bursting with love*
– long-lasting pain based in anxiety –
because I know – this is a sickness –
that if I don't get – if I live –
16 *Morfudd, then life is in vain.*
Heal me – praise of a worthy line –
of my wretchedness and my affliction.
Combine for a year the office of love-messenger
20 *to a girl with the blessings of God.*
No need, unfailing golden image,
for you ever to fear the sin of lust.
God does not undo – good his peace –
24 *what he has done. You shall not fall from heaven.*
No prim maid will see you this year
whispering with us in a narrow space.
Angry, crass-minded Eiddig will not lay
28 *the end of his staff upon you – chaste her mind.*
Come – because of your merits (Quiet!) none will
suspect you, long in the company of virgins –
from Llanddwyn, land often sought,
32 *to Cwm-y-gro, gem of Christendom.*

Llanddwyn

Duw ni'th omeddawdd, hawdd hedd,
Dawn iaith aml, dyn ni'th omedd.
Diamau weddïau waith,
Duw a'th eilw, du ei thalaith.
Delid Duw, dy letywr,
Dêl i gof, dwylaw y gŵr,
Traws oedd y neb a'i treisiai,
Tra ddêl i'm ôl trwy ddail Mai.
Dwynwen, pes parud unwaith
Dan wŷdd Mai a hirddydd maith,
Dawn ei bardd, da, wen, y bych;
Dwynwen, nid oeddud anwych.
Dangos o'th radau dawngoeth
Nad wyd fursen, Ddwynwen ddoeth.

Er a wnaethost yn ddawnbwys
O benyd y byd a'i bwys;
Er y crefydd, ffydd ffyrfryw,
A wnaethost tra fuost fyw;
Er yr eirian leianaeth
A gwyrdawd y coethgnawd caeth;
Er enaid, be rhaid yrhawg,
Brychan Yrth, breichiau nerthawg;
Eiriol er dy greuol gred,
Yr em wyry, roi ymwared.

God did not deny you – easy peace –
the gift of ample speech. No one will deny you.
Beyond doubt God calls you
36 *to the work of prayer – black her headdress.*
May God, your host, constrain –
keep this in mind – her husband's hands.
Cruel would be anyone who would force her,
40 *as she follows me through the May leaves.*
Dwynwen, if you would arrange just once
under the May trees and on a long, long day
a gift for her poet, blessed would you be, fair one.
44 *Dwynwen, you would not be mean.*
Show by your fine gifted blessings
that you are no prim maid, wise Dwynwen.

For the sake of the penance you did, full of grace,
48 *for the world and its weight,*
for the sake of the devotion – strong faith –
you maintained whilst you were alive,
for the sake of your radiant nunhood
52 *and the virginity of your pure oath-bound flesh,*
for the soul's sake – if necessary now –
of Brychan Yrth, strong of arm,
intercede, for the sake of your blood-stained faith,
56 *gem of a virgin, to grant me deliverance.*

Cyngor Gruffudd Gryg i Ddafydd

Gruffudd:
Rhag cyfraith dewfaith, Dafydd – ŵr beius,
  A'r Bwa, llym gigydd,
  Gorau i ti rhag garw oed dydd
  Ymarfer peidio â Morfudd.

Dafydd:
Ni pheidia' â Morfudd, hoff adain – serchog,
  Bes archai Bab Rhufain,
  Hoywliw ddeurudd haul ddwyrain,
  Oni ddêl y mel o'r main.

Gruffudd Gryg's Counsel to Dafydd

Gruffudd:
*Because of the tedious law, Dafydd, guilty man,
    and 'The Bow', keen butcher,
    it's best for you, in case of a rough day's encounter,
    to get used to giving up Morfudd.*

Dafydd:
*I will not give up Morfudd, fond affectionate bird,
    even if the Pope of Rome demanded it,
    cheeks bright-colored as the sun in the east,
    until honey comes from stones.*

Y Don ar Afon Dyfi

Y don bengrychlon grochlais,
Na ludd, goel budd, ym gael bais
I'r tir draw lle daw ym dâl,
Nac oeta fi, nac atal.
Gad, ardwy rhad, er Duw Rhi,
Rhwyfo dwfr rhof a Dyfi.
Tro drachefn, trefn trychanrhwyd,
Dy fardd wyf, uwch dwfr ydd wyd.

A ganodd neb â genau
O fawl i'r twrf meistrawl tau,
Gymar hwyl, gem yr heli,
Gamen môr, gymain â mi?
Ni bu brifwynt planedsygn,
Na rhuthr blawdd na deugawdd dygn,
Nac esgud frwydr nac ysgwr,
Nac ysgwydd gorwydd na gŵr,
Nas cyfflypwn, gwn gyni,
Grefdaer don, i'th gryfder di.
Ni bu organ na thelyn,
Na thafawd difeiwawd dyn,
Nas barnwn yn un gyfref,
Fordwy glas, â'th fawrdeg lef.
Ni chair yr ail gair gennyf
Am f'enaid, brad naid, bryd Nyf,
Ond galw ei thegwch golau
A'i phryd teg yn lle'r ffrwd dau.

The Wave on the River Dyfi

Curly-headed, mighty, loud-voiced wave,
do not prevent me – favorable omen – from finding a crossing
to the land over there where a reward will come to me.
4 Do not delay me, do not restrain me.
Allow me – gracious protection – for the Lord God's sake,
to row over the water between me and the Dyfi.
Turn back, home of 300 nets.
8 I am your poet – you are higher than the water.

Has anyone ever sung with his lips
such praise to your masterful roar,
sail's companion, gem of the brine,
12 curve of the sea, as I?
There was no cardinal wind in any planetary sign,
no tumultuous rush, no grievous double wrath,
no swift battle, no spear,
16 no shoulder of steed or man,
that I would not compare – I know hardship –
strong, fierce wave, to your power.
There was no organ or harp
20 or man's tongue with faultless praise
that I would not judge as strong,
blue surge of the sea, as your great, fair voice.
Not another word from me is to be had
24 about my darling – treacherous fortune – the image of Nyf,
except to compare her bright beauty
and her fair face to your flood.

Tonnau pengrych ar foryd Dyfi ✧ *Curly-headed waves on the Dyfi estuary*

Am hynny, gwna na'm lluddiych,
Ymwanwraig loyw dwfr croyw crych,
I fyned, f'annwyl a'm barn,
Drwy lwyn bedw draw Lanbadarn
At ferch a'm gwnaeth, ffraeth ffrwythlyw,
Forwyn fwyn, o farw yn fyw.
Cyfyng gennyf fy nghyngor,
Cyfeilles, marchoges môr:
Ateg wyd rhof a'm cymwd,
Atal â'th drwyn ffrwyn y ffrwd.
Pei gwypud, don ffalinglwyd,
Pefrgain letywraig aig wyd,
Maint fy ngherydd am drigiaw!
Mantell wyd i'r draethell draw.

Therefore, make sure you do not impede me,
bright jousting-woman of fresh rippling water,
from going – my darling would condemn me –
through the birch grove beyond Llanbadarn
to a girl who brought me – a fluent fruitful lord,
a gentle maiden – from death back to life.
Perilous is my predicament,
friend, horsewoman of the sea:
you are a barrier between me and my commot.
Curb the flood with your bridle.
If only you knew, grey-mantled wave,
– you are the bright, beautiful hostess of the sea –
the magnitude of my rebuke for my delay!
You are a mantle over yonder shore.

28
32
36
40

Dŵr llwyd afon Dyfi ger Machynlleth ✧ *The Dyfi in spate near Machynlleth*

Cyd deuthum er ail Indeg
Hyd yn dy fron, y don deg,
Ni'm lladdo rhyfel gelyn
O'm lluddiud i dud y dyn;
Neu'm lladd saith ugeinradd serch,
Na'm lludd at Forfudd, f'eurferch.

Though I have come for the sake of a second Indeg
as far as your breast, fair wave,
no enemy's war will slay me
44 *if you should keep me from the girl's land:*
the seven score degrees of love shall slay me.
Do not keep me from Morfudd, my golden girl!

Taith i Garu

A gerddodd neb er gordderch
A gerddais i, gorddwy serch,
Rhew ac eiry, rhyw garedd,
Glaw a gwynt er gloyw ei gwedd?   4
Ni chefais eithr nych ofwy.
Ni chafas deudroed hoed hwy
Ermoed i Gellïau'r Meirch,
Eurdrais elw, ar draws Eleirch   8
Yn anial dir, yn uniawn
Nos a dydd, ac nid nes dawn.

Love's Journey

Did anyone ever walk for a lover
as I have walked – love's tyranny –
through ice and snow – a kind of passion –
rain and wind, for one with her radiant form?
I got nothing but a bout of torment.
Two feet never got greater grief
going to Cellïau'r Meirch
– profit of a fine effort – across Eleirch
in the wilderness, unswerving
night and day, with reward no nearer.

Bwlch Meibion Dafydd, Cwm-y-glo, Elerch

42

O! Dduw, ys uchel o ddyn
Ei floedd yng Nghelli Fleddyn:
Ymadrodd er ei mwyn hi,
Ymarddelw o serch bûm erddi.
Bysaleg iselgreg sôn,
Berwgau lif bergul afon,
Mynych iawn er ei mwyn hi
Y treiddiwn beunydd trwyddi.
I Fwlch yr awn yn falch rydd,
Mau boen dwfn, Meibion Dafydd,
Ac ymaith draw i'r Gamallt
Ac i'r Rhiw er gwiw ei gwallt.
Ebrwydd y cyrchwn o'r blaen
Gyfaelfwlch y Gyfylfaen
I fwrw am forwyn wisgra
Dremyn ar y dyffryn da.
Ni thry nac yma na thraw
Hebof yn lledrad heibiaw.
Ystig fûm ac anaraf
Ar hyd Pont Cwcwll yr haf
A gogylch Castell Gwgawn—
Gogwydd cyw gŵydd lle câi gawn.
Rhedais heb adail Heilin
Rhediad bloesg fytheiad blin.
Sefais goris llys Ifor
Fal manach mewn cilfach côr
I geisio heb addo budd
Gyfarfod â gwiw Forfudd.
Nid oes dwyn na dwys dyno
Yn neutu glyn Nant-y-glo
Nas medrwyf o'm nwyf a'm nydd
Heb y llyfr, hoywbwyll Ofydd.

Oh, God! Loud was a man's
12 cry in Celli Fleddyn,
calling out because of her;
I was professing love for her.
Bysaleg's murmuring sound,
16 the bubbling flow of a short narrow stream,
quite often for her sake
I would cross over every day.
I would go to Bwlch – proud and free,
20 deep pain is mine – Meibion Dafydd,
and away over to Y Gamallt
and to Y Rhiw for the one with lovely hair.
Swiftly I would make for the top of
24 Gyfaelfwlch y Gyfylfaen
to get, for the sake of a fur-clad maiden,
a view of the fine valley.
She cannot, either here or there,
28 get past stealthily without me.
I was persistent and quick
along Pont Cwcwll in the summer
and around Castell Gwgawn,
32 a goose chick bending forward to get rushes.
I ran past Heilyn's house,
the run of a tired, stammering hound.
I stood below Ifor's court
36 like a monk in a corner of the choir
to try, without promise of success,
to meet with lovely Morfudd.
There is no hill or deep hollow
40 on either side of Glyn Nant-y-glo
that I don't know, from my passion and pain,
by heart – Ovid's lively temperament.

Afon Bysaleg (Stewi), uwch Cwm-y-glo ✧ *The Bysaleg (Stewi), above Cwm-y-glo*

Hawdd ym wrth leisio i'm dwrn	*Easy for me, crying into my fist,*
Gwir nod helw Gwernytalwrn	44 *to gain the true goal at Gwernytalwrn,*
Lle cefais weled, ged gu,	*a place where I could see, precious gift,*
Llerwddyn dan fantell orddu,	*a slender girl under a dark black mantle,*
Lle gwelir yn dragywydd,	*a place where there can always be seen,*
Heb dwf gwellt, heb dyfu gwŷdd,	48 *with no growth of grass, no trees growing,*
Llun ein gwâl dan wial da,	*the impression of our couch under fine saplings,*
Lle briwddail, fal llwybr Adda.	*a place of broken leaves, like Adam's path.*
Gwae ef, yr enaid, heb sâl	*Woe to the soul, without reward*
Rhag blinder, heb gwbl undal,	52 *for its weariness, without any payment at all,*
O thry yr unffordd achlân	*if it wanders about the very same way*
Y tröes y corff truan.	*as the wretched body wandered.*

Dyddgu

Ynys Aberteifi oddi waered Fferm Tywyn ✧ *Cardigan Island from below Tywyn Farm*

Dyddgu

Ieuan, iôr gwaywdan gwiwdad,
Iawnfab Gruffudd, cythrudd cad,
Fab Llywelyn, wyn wingaer,
Llwyd, unben wyd, iawnben aer,
Y nos arall, naws arial,
Y bûm i'th dŷ. Bo maith dâl.
Nid hawdd er hyn hyd heddiw,
Hoen wymp, ym gaffael hun wiw.
Dy aur a gawn rhadlawn rhydd,
Dy loyw win, dy lawenydd,
Dy fedd glas, difaddau i glêr,
Dy fragod du ei friger.

Dy ferch, gwn na ordderchai,
Feinwen deg, o'th faenwyn dai.
Ni chysgais, ni weais wawd,
Hun na'i dryll, heiniau drallawd.
Duw lwyd,—pwy a'm dilidia?—
Dim yn fy nghalon nid â
Eithr ei chariad taladwy.
O rhoid ym oll, ai rhaid mwy?
Ni'm câr hon. Neu'm curia haint.
Ni'm gad hun o'm gad henaint.

Rhyfedd gan Ddoethion Rhufain
Rhyfedded pryd fy myd main.
Gwynnach yw nog eiry gwanwyn.
Gweddw wyf o serch y ferch fwyn.
Gwyn yw'r tâl dan wialen,
Du yw'r gwallt, diwair yw gwen.
Duach yw'r gwallt, diochr gwŷdd,
No mwyalch neu gae mywydd.
Gwynder disathr ar lathrgnawd
Yn duo'r gwallt, iawnder gwawd.

Dyddgu

Ieuan – fiery-speared lord of worthy descent –
true son of Gruffudd – inciter of battle –
son of Llywelyn – with a white wine-fort –
4 Llwyd, you are a chieftain, a true war leader.
The other night, in a lively mood,
I was at your house. May there be great reward!
It has not been easy since then until today
8 – great gladness – for me to get proper sleep.
Your gold I received, generous gift,
your bright wine, your joy,
your fresh mead, ever abundant for poets,
12 your bragget, black its foam.

Your daughter, I know she would not be a lover,
fair and slender, from your white stone court.
I've not slept – I've not woven a song –
16 a wink of sleep, troublesome sickness.
Holy God! Who will calm me down?
Nothing enters my heart
but her precious love.
20 If all were given to me, would I need more?
She doesn't love me. Sickness wastes me away.
She won't let me sleep, even if I reach old age.

It would be a wonder to the Wise Men of Rome
24 how wondrous is the face of my slender darling.
She is whiter than spring snow.
I am bereft from love of the gentle maiden.
White is the forehead below her braid,
28 black is the hair, the fair girl is chaste.
Blacker is the hair – the strands straight –
Than a blackbird or a clasp of jet,
Absolute whiteness on smooth skin
32 makes the hair blacker – proper for praise.

46

Nid annhebig, ddiddig ddydd,
Modd ei phryd, medd ei phrydydd,
I'r ferch hygar a garawdd
Y milwr gynt, mau lwyr gawdd,
Peredur, ddwysgur ddisgwyl,
Fab Efrog, gwrdd farchog gŵyl,
Pan oedd yn edrych, wych wawl,
Yn yr eiry, iôn eryrawl,
Llen asur, ger llwyn Esyllt,
Llwybr balch, lle buasai'r gwalch gwyllt
Yn lladd, heb neb a'i lluddiai,
Mwyalch, morwyn falch ar fai.
Yno'r oedd iawn arwyddion–
Pand Duw a'i tâl?–peintiad hon:
Mewn eiry gogyfuwch luwch lwyth
Modd ei thâl, medd ei thylwyth.
Asgell y fwyalch esgud
Megis ei hael. Megais hud.
Gwaed yr edn gwedy r'odi,
Gradd haul, mal ei gruddiau hi.
Felly mae, eurgae organ,
Dyddgu a'r gwallt gloywddu glân.

Beirniad fûm gynt hynt hyntiaw.
Barned rhawd o'r beirniaid draw
Ai hywaith, fy nihewyd,
Ymy fy myw am fy myd.

Her look, her poet says,
is not unlike – pleasant day –
the lovable girl who was loved by
36 *the warrior of old – complete suffering is mine –*
Peredur – observing in deep anguish –
son of Efrog – brave and modest knight –
when he was looking, splendid brightness,
40 *in the snow – eagle-like lord,*
in an azure cloak, by Essyllt's grove –
at a splendid print, where the wild hawk had been
killing, with none to prevent it,
44 *a blackbird – a proud maiden is to blame.*
There were the proper elements
– Isn't it God who pays for it? – of her visage:
In snow as high as a great snowdrift
48 *is the look of her forehead, say her kin.*
The wing of the swift blackbird
Is like her eyebrow. I am spellbound.
The bird's blood after it had snowed,
52 *bright as the sun, is like her cheeks.*
Such is – gold-clasped organ –
Dyddgu and her lustrous pure black hair.

I was once a critic wandering about.
56 *Let yonder crowd of critics decide:*
Is it worth it – she is my ardent desire –
for me, my living in longing for my love?

Gwahodd Dyddgu

Dyn cannaid doniog gynneddf,
Dyddgu â'r gwallt lliwddu lleddf,
Dy wahawdd, cawddnawdd cuddnwyf,
I ddôl Mynafon ydd wyf.
Nid gwahodd gwyw a'th gydfydd,
Nid gwahodd glwth i'i fwth fydd.
Nid gorchwy elw medelwas,
Nid o ŷd, gloyw amyd glas.
Nid tam o ginio amaeth,
Ac nid ynyd ciglyd caeth.
Nid gofwy Sais â'i gyfaillt,
Nid neithior arf barf mab aillt.
Nid addawaf, da ddiwedd,
I'm aur ond eos a medd;
Eos gefnllwyd ysgafnllef
A bronfraith ddigrifiaith gref,
Ygus dwf, ac ystafell
O fedw ir; a fu dŷ well?
Tra fôm allan dan y dail
Ein ceinnerth fedw a'n cynnail.
Llofft i'r adar i chwarae,
Llwyn mwyn, llyna'r llun y mae.
Nawpren teg eu hwynepryd
Y sydd o goedwydd i gyd:
I waered yn grwm gwmpas,
I fyny yn glochdy glas.
A thanun', eiddun addef,
Meillion ir, ymellin nef.
Lle deuddyn, llu a'u diddawr,
Neu dri yn ennyd yr awr.
Lle y cyrch rhywiociyrch rhiw,
Lle cân edn, lle cain ydiw.
Lle tew lletyau mwyeilch,
Lle mygr gwŷdd, lle megir gweilch.
Lle newydd adeilwydd da,
Lle nwyf aml, lle nef yma.

An Invitation for Dyddgu

Radiant girl of a gifted nature,
Dyddgu with the smooth black hair,
I invite you – hidden desire is anger's refuge –
4   to the vale of Minafon.
No feeble invitation would suit you.
No greedy man's invitation to his shack will it be.
No provisions for the benefit of a young reaper,
8   no corn, bright green mixed corn,
no bit of a ploughman's dinner,
and no meaty feast of a serf,
no Englishman's visit with his friend,
12   no razor celebration of a bondman.
No promise will I make – a good ending –
to my golden one but a nightingale and mead,
a light-voiced brown-backed nightingale
16   and a thrush with hearty, pleasant speech,
shaded growth, and a chamber
of verdant birch. Was there ever a better house?
While we are out under the leaves
20   our fine strong birch will guard us.
A loft for the birds to play in,
a pleasant grove – that's the way it is.
Nine trees of fair appearance
24   are in the wood altogether:
at the bottom, a rounded circumference;
at the top, a green bell tower.
And beneath them – desirable dwelling –
28   verdant clover – manna from heaven –
a place where two – a crowd worries them –
or three can spend an hour or so,
a place where noble roebucks come from the hill,
32   a place where birds sing – it is a fine place –
a place of dense blackbird dwellings,
a place of splendid trees, a place hawks are reared,
a place of good new building-trees,
36   a place of great desire, a place of heaven on earth,

48

Afon Rheidol ar hyd Dôl Minafon ✧ *The Rheidol along Dôl Minafon*

Lle golas rwyl, lle gŵyl gwg,
Lle gyr dwfr, lle goer difwg.
Lle nid hysbys, dyrys dir,
Blotai neu gawsai goesir.
Yno heno, hoen gwaneg,
Awn ni ein dau, fy nyn deg,
Awn, od awn, wyneb gwynhoyw,
Fy nyn lygad glöyn gloyw.

a place with a green mansion, a place frowns are mild,
a place near water, a cool smoke-free place,
a place not well-known – thickly wooded land –
40 *to flour merchants and long-legged cheese makers.*
There tonight, wave's brightness,
let us go, the two of us, my fair girl,
let us go, if we go anywhere, lively one fair of face,
44 *my girl with eyes bright as coals.*

Y Gainc

Dysgais ryw baradwysgainc
Â'r dwylo mau ar dâl mainc,
A'r dysgiad, diwygiad dyn,
Eurai dalm ar y delyn.
Llyma'r gainc ar y fainc fau,
O blith oed yn blethiadau
O deilyngfawl edlingferch
A brydais i â brwyd serch.

Meddai ferched y gwledydd
Amdanaf fi, o'm dawn fydd:
'Semlen yw hon naws amlwg,
A symlyn yw'r dyn a'i dwg.'

Solffeais, o'm salw ffuaint,
Salm rwydd, ys aelaw 'y mraint,
Ac erddigan gan y gainc
Garuaidd, medd gwyreainc.
Coel fuddbwnc ferw celfyddber,
Cael ym glod, neud cwlm y glêr,
Caniadlais edn caneidlon,
Cân a fyn beirdd heirdd yw hon.

Gwae fi na chlyw, mawr yw'r ainc,
Dyddgu hyn o brydyddgainc.
Os byw, hi a'i clyw uwch clwyd
Ysbyslef eos beislwyd,
O ddysg Hildr oddis cildant,
Gormodd cerdd, gŵr meddw a'i cant;
Llef eurloyw fygr llafurlais,
Lleddf ddatbing llwybr sawtring Sais.
Ni wnaeth pibydd ffraeth o Ffrainc
Na phencerdd ryw siffancainc.

The Tune

I learned a heavenly tune
with my own hands at the end of the bench,
and that learning – a man's custom –
gilded the harp for a while.
Here is the tune on my bench
from the midst of a tryst, the interweavings
of a noble girl's well-deserved praise,
which I composed on love's loom.

The girls around the countryside say
about me, because of my talent,
'This is a simple thing with an obvious form,
and the one who brings it is a simpleton.'

I sol-fa-ed, with my foolish pretence,
an easy psalm – abundant is my privilege –
and harmony along with that lovely
tune, the boys say.
Portent of a profitable song, sweet and skilful,
bringing me praise, the minstrels' melody,
the tuneful voice of a bright, joyful bird,
this is a song that handsome poets wish for.

Alas that Dyddgu – great is the desire –
Cannot hear this poet's tune!
If she lives, she will hear it above the perch
of a clear-noted, grey-coated nightingale
with Hildr's skill below the treble string,
an excess of song – a drunken man sang it,
the fine gold-bright note of a laboured voice,
the plaintive notes of an Englishman's psaltery.
No fluent piper from France,
no chief musician ever made such a tune.

Poed anolo fo ei fin,
A'i gywydd a'i ddeg ewin,
A gano cerdd ogoniant,
Ni cherydd Duw, na cherdd dant,
Goleuglaer ddyn golyglon,
Ac e'n cael canu'r gainc hon.

Let his mouth be worthless
32 *and his* cywydd *and his ten nails,*
he who might sing a song of praise
– God will not blame him – or play a harp song
for a clear, bright, glad-eyed girl
36 *when he could play this tune.*

Merched Heb Eu Henwi ✧ Unnamed Girls

Eglwys Llanbadarn Fawr ✧ Llanbadarn Fawr church

Merched Llanbadarn

Plygu rhag llid yr ydwyf,
Pla ar holl ferched y plwyf!
Am na chefais, drais drawsoed,
Ohonun yr un erioed,
Na morwyn, fwyn ofynaig,
Na merch fach na gwrach na gwraig.
Pa rusiant, pa ddireidi,
Pa fethiant na fynnant fi?
Pa ddrwg i riain feinael
Yng nghoed tywylldew fy nghael?
Nid oedd gywilydd iddi
Yng ngwâl dail fy ngweled i.

Ni bu amser na charwn —
Ni bu mor lud hud â hwn —
Anad gwyr annwyd Garwy,
Yn y dydd ai un ai dwy,
Ac er hynny nid oedd nes
Ym gael un no'm gelynes.
Ni bu Sul yn Llanbadarn
Na bewn, ac eraill a'i barn,
A'm wyneb at y ferch goeth
A'm gwegil at Dduw gwiwgoeth.
A chwedy'r hir edrychwyf
Dros fy mhlu ar draws fy mhlwyf,
Syganai y fun befrgroyw
Wrth y llall hylwyddgall, hoyw:

'Godinabus fydd golwg —
Gŵyr ei ddrem gelu ei ddrwg —
Y mab llwyd wyneb mursen
A gwallt ei chwaer ar ei ben.'

The Girls of Llanbadarn

I am doubled over with anger,
– a plague on all the girls of the parish! –
because I have not had – mighty oppressive longing –
4   a single one of them ever,
neither maiden – a gentle request –
nor young girl nor old woman nor wife.
What is the reluctance, what mischief,
8   what failing, that they do not want me?
What harm to a slender-browed maiden
To have me in a dense dark wood?
It would be no shame for her
12   to see me in a bed of leaves.

There never was a time I did not love,
– there never was such lasting enchantment as this –
even more than men with Garwy's ardour,
16   either one or two a day,
and despite that, I was no nearer
to getting one than if she were my enemy.
There was no Sunday in Llanbadarn
20   that I would not be – and others condemn it –
with my face towards a splendid girl
and the nape of my neck towards most splendid God.
And after I have been looking a long time
24   over my feathers at my parish,
the sweet, bright maiden would whisper
to the other, lively, wise, prosperous:

'Lascivious is the look
28   – his eye knows how to hide his wickedness –
of the pale lad with the face of a flirt
and his sister's hair on his head.'

'Ai'n rhith hynny yw ganthaw?'
Yw gair y llall geir ei llaw,
'Ateb nis caiff tra fo byd,
Wtied i ddiawl, beth ynfyd!'

Talmithr ym rheg y loywferch,
Tâl bychan am syfrdan serch.
Rhaid oedd ym fedru peidiaw
Â'r foes hon, breuddwydion braw.
Gorau ym fyned fal gŵr
Yn feudwy, swydd anfadwr.
O dra disgwyl, dysgiad certh,
Drach 'y nghefn, drych anghyfnerth,
Neur dderyw ym, gerddrym gâr,
Bengamu heb un gymar.

32   'Is that the way it is with him?'
says the other beside her.
'He shall get no response while the world lasts.
Let him hoot to the devil, daft thing!'

Harsh to me the bright girl's 'gift',
36   *small recompense for giddy love.*
I must try to cease
this behavior, dreadful dreams.
Best for me to become someone
40   *like a hermit, a scoundrel's role.*
From too much looking – a true lesson –
over my shoulder – a sorry sight –
I have become – a friend powerful in song –
44   *stiff-necked, without any companion.*

Cusan

Hawddamawr, ddeulawr ddilyth,
Haeddai fawl, i heddiw fyth,
Yn rhagorol, dwyol daith,
Rhag doe neu echdoe nychdaith.
Nid oedd debig, Ffrengig ffriw,
Dyhuddiant doe i heddiw.
Nid un wawd, neud anwadal,
Heddiw â doe, hoywdda dâl.
Ie, Dduw Dad, a ddaw dydd
Unlliw â heddiw hoywddydd?
Heddiw y cefais hoywddawn,
Her i ddoe, hwyr yw ei ddawn.

Cefais werth, gwnaeth ym chwerthin,
Canswllt a morc, cwnsallt min.
Cusan fu ym (cyson wyf fi)
Cain Luned, can oleuni.
Celennig lerw ddierwin,
Clyw, er Mair, clo ar y min.
Ceidw ynof serch y ferch fad,
Coel mawr gur, cwlm ar gariad.
Cof a ddaw ynof i'w ddwyn,
Ciried mawr, cariad morwyn.
Coron am ganon genau,
Caerfyrddin cylch y min mau.
Cain bacs min diorwacserch,
Cwlm hardd rhwng meinfardd a merch.
Cynneddf hwn neb niw cennyw,
Cynnadl dau anadl, da yw.
Cefais, ac wi o'r cyfoeth,
Corodyn min dyn mwyn, doeth.

A Kiss

Hail – unequaled, unfailing,
praiseworthy – to today forever,
surpassing – divine journey –
4 *the grievous journey of yesterday or the day before!*
Yesterday's consolation was not like
today's – with a French aspect to it.
Not the same song of praise – it is fickle –
8 *today as yesterday – exquisite payment.*
Indeed, God the Father, will there ever come a day
the same colour as this exquisite day?
Today I received an exquisite gift.
12 *Away with yesterday! Its gift is too late.*

I received the value – it made me laugh –
of 100 shillings and a mark – a mouth's mantle.
There was a kiss for me – I am constant –
16 *from fair Luned, brilliant light.*
A New-Year's gift, dainty, not rough,
hear me, by Mary, a lock on the lips!
It keeps in me the love of the fine lass
20 *– portent of great pain – a love knot.*
The memory comes to me of bearing it
– great generosity – a maiden's love.
A crown about the mouth's canon,
24 *Carmarthen castle encircling my mouth.*
A fine kiss-of-peace from true love's lips,
a beautiful bond between a slender poet and a maid.
No one can know the remarkable qualities of this:
28 *the meeting together of two breaths. It is good.*
I got – and Oh, the riches! –
a trifle from the lips of a wise, gentle girl.

'Caerfyrddin cylch y min mau.' ✧ *'Carmarthen castle encircling my mouth.'*

56

Cryf wyf o'i gael yn ael nod,
Crair min disglair mwyn dwysglod.
Criaf ei wawd, ddidlawd ddadl,
Crynais gan y croyw anadl.
Cwlm cariad mewn tabliad dwbl,
Cwmpasgaer min campusgwbl.

Cyd cefais, ddidrais ddwydrin,
Heiniar mawl, hwn ar 'y min,
Trysor ym yw, trisawr mêl,
Teiroch ym os caiff Turel,
Ac os caiff hefyd, bryd brau,
Mursen fyth, mawrson fwythau.
Ni bu ddrwg, ei gwg a gaf,
Lai no dwrn Luned arnaf.

Inseiliodd a haeddodd hi,
Mul oeddwn, fy mawl iddi.
Ni ddaw o'm tafawd wawdair
Mwy er merch, berw serch a bair,
Eithr a ddêl, uthrwedd wylan,
Ar fy nghred, i Luned lân.
Eiddun anadl cariadloes,
A Dduw, mwy a ddaw i'm oes
Y rhyw ddydd, heulwenddydd wiw,
Am hoywddyn, ym â heddiw?

I am strong from getting it on the brink of success,
32 *a treasure of bright, gentle lips, highly praised.*
I proclaim its praise, unstinting deliberation,
I trembled with that sweet breath,
a love knot in double form,
36 *encircling fortress of a most excellent mouth.*

Though I got – double contention without strife,
harvest of praise – this on my lips
– it is a treasure to me, three scents of honey –
40 *thrice woe to me if Turel gets it,*
and also if – feeble mind –
a strumpet with widely-known caresses ever gets it.
It was no bad thing – her frown I shall get –
44 *something less than Luned's fist on me.*

She put her seal on and she deserved
– I was sincere – my praise of her.
No greater word of praise shall come from my tongue
48 *for a girl – boiling love causes it –*
except what may come – wondrous seagull's form –
by my faith, to fair Luned.
Desirable breath of love's pain,
52 *Ah, God! Will there come to me again in my life*
such a day – a fine, sunny day
because of an exquisite girl – as today?

Y Deildy

Heirdd feirdd, f'eurddyn, diledfeirw,
Hawddamor, hoen goror geirw,
I fun lwys a'm cynhwysai
Mewn bedw a chyll, mentyll Mai,
Llathr daerfalch, uwch llethr derfyn,
Lle da i hoffi lliw dyn.
Gwir ddodrefn o'r gaer ddidryf,
Gwell yw ystafell a dyf.

The House of Leaves

Lovely lively poets, greet my golden one
– bright hue of the roiling seashore –
the beautiful maiden who would welcome me
amongst birch and hazel, May's mantles,
resplendent, eager and proud, above a slope's edge,
a good place to delight in a girl's complexion.
True furnishings of the solitary fortress,
better is a room that grows.

4

8

Bedwenni, Cwm Elan ✧ *Birches, Elan Valley*

58

O daw meinwar, fy nghariad,
I dŷ dail a wnaeth Duw Dad,
Dyhuddiant fydd y gwydd gwiw,
Dihuddygl o dŷ heddiw.
Nid gwaeth gorwedd dan gronglwyd;
Nid gwaeth deiliadaeth Duw lwyd.
Unair wyf fi â'm cyfoed.
Yno y cawn yn y coed
Clywed siarad gan adar,
Clerwyr coed, claerwawr a'u câr:
Cywyddau, gweau gwiail,
Cywion, priodolion dail;
Cenedl â dychwedl dichwerw,
Cywion cerddorion caer dderw.

Dewin fy nhŷ a'i dawnha,
Dwylo Mai a'i hadeila,
A'i linyn yw'r gog lonydd
A'i ysgwâr yw eos gwŷdd,
A'i dywydd yw hirddydd haf
A'i ais yw goglais gwiwglaf,
Ac allor serch yw'r gelli
Yn gall, a'i fwyall wyf fi.
Nachaf yn nechrau blwyddyn
Yn hwy y tyf no hyd dyn.

Pell i'm bryd roddi gobrau
I wrach o hen gilfach gau.
Ni cheisiaf, adroddaf drais,
Wrth adail a wrthodais.

If a slender gentle girl, my darling,
will come to a house of leaves God the Father made,
the excellent trees will provide solace,
12 *a soot-free house today.*
No worse lying under such a roof.
No worse such a tenancy under holy God.
I am of the same mind as my companion:
16 *There in the wood we can*
listen to the birds reciting
– the poets of the wood (the bright lady loves them) –
the cywyddau, *in the woven branches,*
20 *of the chicks, residents of the leaves,*
a kindred with a sweet tale,
the musician chicks of the oaken fortress.

God shall endow my house,
24 *May's hands shall build it,*
and its plumb-line is the tranquil cuckoo,
and its square is the nightingale of the wood,
and its framework is the long summer day,
28 *and its laths are the pangs of the love-sick,*
and the grove is an altar of love,
wisely, and I am its axe.
Behold, in the beginning of the year
32 *it grows taller than a man's height.*

Far from my mind is paying a reward
To a hag of an old hollow nook.
I will not seek anything – I speak of betrayal –
36 *from the building which I have forsaken.*

Caru'n Ddiffrwyth

Ei serch a roes merch i mi,
Seren cylch Nantyseri,
Morwyn wych, nid ym marn au,
Morfudd ŵyl, mawr feddyliau.
Cyd collwyf o wiwnwyf uthr
Fy anrhaith a fu iawnrhuthr,
Cyd bu brid ein newid ni,
Prid oedd i'r priod eiddi.
Eithr rhag anfodd, uthr geinfyw,
Duw fry, diedifar yw,
Gwedy i'i chariad brad fu'r braw,
Lloer byd, rhoi llw ar beidiaw.

O cherais wraig mewn meigoel
Wrth lyn y porthmonyn moel,
Gwragennus esgus osgordd,
Gwraig, rhyw benaig, Robin Nordd,
Elen chwannog i olud,
Fy anrhaith â'r lediaith lud,
Brenhines, arglwyddes gwlân,
Brethyndai bro eithindan,
Dyn serchog oedd raid yno.
Gwae hi nad myfi fai fo!
Ni chymer hon, wiwdon wedd,
Gerdd yn rhad, gwrdd anrhydedd.
Hawdd oedd gael, gafael gyfa',
Haws no dim, hosanau da.
Ac os caf liw gwynnaf gwawn,
O fedlai y'm gwnâi'n fodlawn.

Loving in Vain

A girl gave her love to me,
the star of the region around Nantyseri,
splendid maiden – no false judgement –
4 gentle Morfudd – great memories.
Though I shall lose, from dreadful great desire,
my prize who was truly impetuous,
though our exchange was costly,
8 it was costly to that husband of hers.
But in the face of the displeasure – dreadful proper living –
of God above, she is without regret
– afterwards the shock was a betrayal to her lover –
12 the world's moon, for swearing an oath to stop.

If I loved a woman with some confidence
over a drink from the bald little merchant,
bent-backed, with a poor excuse for a following,
16 the wife of – sort of a lord – Robin Nordd,
Elen, eager for riches,
my prize with the strong accent,
lady of wool, queen
20 of the cloth-houses of the region of fiery gorse,
a loving man was a necessity there.
Alas for her that it is not me!
She, with the look of a lovely wave, will not accept
24 a poem for free, as a matter of great honour.
It was easy getting – full possession,
easier than anything – good hosiery.
And if I get her of the whitest gossamer hue,
28 she would make me content with motley.

Nantyseri

Nid ydwyf, nwyf anofal,
Rho Duw, heb gaffael rhyw dâl
Ai ar eiriau arwyrain
Ai ar feddwl cerddgar cain,
Ai â'r aur, cyd diheurwyf,
Ai ar ryw beth. Arab wyf.
Hefyd cyd bo fy nhafawd
I Ddyddgu yn gwëu gwawd,
Nid oes ym, myn Duw, o swydd
Ond olrhain anwadalrhwydd.

Gwawr brenhiniaeth, maeth â'i medd,
Y byd ŵyr, yw'r bedwaredd.
Ni chaiff o'm pen cymen call,
Hoen geirw, na hi nac arall
Na'i henw na'r wlad yr hanoedd,
Hoff iawn yw, na pha un oedd.
Nid oes na gwraig, benaig nwyf,
Na gŵr cimin a garwyf
Â'r forwyn glaer galchgaer gylch.
Nos da iddi nis diylch.
Cair gair o garu'n ddiffrwyth.
Caf, nid arbedaf fi, bwyth.

Be gwypai, gobaith undyn,
Mae amdani hi fai hyn,
Bai cynddrwg, geinwen rudd-deg,
Genthi â'i chrogi wych reg.
Mwy lawnbwys mau elynboen,
Moli a wnaf hi, Nyf hoen,
Hoyw ei llun, a holl Wynedd
A'i mawl. Gwyn ei fyd a'i medd!

I have always – carefree desire –
by God, received some payment,
either for words of praise
32   *or fine melodious thought,*
either with gold – though I would excuse myself –
or with something. I am witty.
Also, though my tongue may be
36   *weaving praise for Dyddgu,*
there is nothing for me, by God, to do
except to keep track of her fickleness.

A princess of the kingdom, raised on its mead,
40   *the world knows, is the fourth.*
Neither she, foam's brightness, nor another
will get from my wise discreet mouth,
either her name or the land she comes from
44   *– she is very lovely – or which one she was.*
There is neither woman, chief of desire,
nor man that I love as much
as the lime-white-fort-bright maiden.
48   *Say 'Good night' to her: no thanks for it.*
They speak of loving in vain.
I shall get – I will not refrain – a reward.

If she knew – one man's hope –
52   *that this was about her,*
such a splendid gift would be as odious to her
– fair-cheeked beauty – as being hanged!
More burdensome this cruel pain of mine,
56   *yet I will praise her, brightness of Nyf,*
– lively her image – and all Gwynedd
praises her. Blessed is he who wins her!

'A holl Wynedd a'i mawl' (Eryri) ✧ 'And all Gwynedd praises her' (Snowdonia)

Trafferth mewn Tafarn

Deuthum i ddinas dethol
A'm hardd wreang i'm hôl.
Cain hoywdraul, lle cwyn hydrum,
Cymryd, balch o febyd fûm,
Llety, urddedig ddigawn,
Cyffredin, a gwin a gawn.
Canfod rhiain addfeindeg
Yn y tŷ, f'un enaid teg.
Bwrw yn llwyr, liw haul dwyrain,
Fy mryd ar wyn fy myd main,
Prynu rhost, nid er bostiaw,
A gwin drud, mi a gwen draw.
Gwaraeau a gâr gwŷr ieuainc,
Galw ar fun, ddyn gŵyl, i'r fainc,
A gwledd am anrhydedd mawr
A wnaethom, mwy no neithiawr.
Hustyng, bûm ŵr hy astud,
Dioer yw hyn, deuair o hud.
Gwedy myned, dynged yng,
Y rhwystr gwedy'r hustyng,
Gwneuthur, ni bu segur serch,
Amod dyfod at hoywferch
Pan elai y minteioedd
I gysgu; bun aelddu oedd.

Trouble at an Inn

I came to a choice town,
with my handsome page behind me.
Fine cheerful expense – an excellent place for dinner –
4 I took – I was a proud youth –
public – dignified enough –
lodging, and I got some wine.
I spied a slim pretty maiden
8 in the house, my one fair friend.
Completely setting – colour of the sun in the east –
my mind on the desire of my slender dear,
I bought a roast – not just for boasting –
12 and expensive wine for me and that lovely girl.
Young men love to play games.
I called the maid, modest girl, to the bench,
and we had a glorious great feast,
16 greater than a wedding banquet.
I whispered – I was a bold, eager fellow,
that's for sure – two words to charm her.
After any obstacle – dire destiny –
20 had been removed by that whispering,
I made – love was not idle –
an agreement to come to the sprightly girl
when the crowds had gone
24 to sleep. She was a black-browed maid.

Gwedy cysgu, tru tremyn,
O bawb onid mi a bun,
Ceisiais yn hyfedr fedru
Ar wely'r ferch, alar fu.
Cefais, pan soniais yna,
Gwymp dig, nid oedd gampau da.
Briwais, ni neidiais yn iach,
Y grimog, a gwae'r omach,
Wrth ystlys, ar waith ostler,
Ystôl groch ffôl, goruwch ffêr.
Trewais, drwg fydd tra awydd,
Lle y'm rhoed, heb un llam rhwydd,
Mynych dwyll amwyll ymwrdd,
Fy nhalcen wrth ben y bwrdd,
Lle'r oedd cawg yrhawg yn rhydd
A llafar badell efydd.
Syrthio o'r bwrdd, dragwrdd drefn,
A'r ddeudrestl a'r holl ddodrefn.
Rhoi diasbad o'r badell,
I'm hôl y'i clywid ymhell.
Gweiddi, gŵr gorwag oeddwn,
O'r cawg, a chyfarth o'r cŵn.

Haws codi, drygioni drud,
Yn drwsgl nog yn dra esgud.
Dyfod, bu chwedl edifar,
I fyny, Cymry a'm câr,
Lle'r oedd garllaw muroedd mawr
Drisais mewn gwely drewsawr
Yn trafferth am eu triphac,
Hicin a Siencin a Siac.
Syganai'r delff soeg enau,
Aruthr o ddig, wrth y ddau:

After everyone – it was extremely pitiful –
went to sleep except me and the girl,
I cleverly tried to make
28 for the girl's bed – it was lamentable.
I got, when I made a noise there,
a nasty fall – these were no fortunate exploits.
I bruised – I did not jump unhurt –
32 my shin – and woe to my leg! –
on the edge – some ostler's work –
of a stupid noisy stool, above the ankle.
I struck – excessive desire is bad –
36 where I landed, without a single leap clear,
– frequent the treachery of foolish struggling –
my forehead on the end of the table,
where there was now a loose basin
40 and a resounding brass bowl.
The table fell – a mighty piece of furniture –
with its two trestles and all the utensils.
The bowl gave a cry
44 behind me which could be heard far away.
The basin – I was a stupid man –
rang out, and the dogs barked.

It's easier to get up – costly mischief –
48 clumsily than too quickly.
I rose – it was a regrettable tale –
up – Welshmen love me! –
where there were, by massive walls,
52 three Englishmen in a stinky bed
worrying about their three packs,
Hickin and Jenkin and Jack.
One slobber-mouthed dimwit whispered,
56 terribly angry, to the other two:

'Mae Cymro, taer gyffro twyll,
Yn rhodio yma'n rhydwyll;
Lleidr yw ef, os goddefwn,
'Mogelwch, cedwch rhag hwn.'

Codi o'r ostler niferoedd
I gyd, a chwedl dybryd oedd.
Gygus oeddynt i'm gogylch
Bob naw i'm ceisiaw o'm cylch,
A minnau, hagr wyniau hyll,
Yn tewi yn y tywyll.
Gweddïais, nid gwedd eofn,
Dan gêl, megis dyn ag ofn,
Ac o nerth gweddi gerth gu,
Ac o ras y gwir Iesu,
Cael i minnau, cwlm anun,
Heb sâl, fy henwal fy hun.
Dihengais i, da yng saint,
I Dduw'r archaf faddeuaint.

'There's a Welshman – deceit's fierce tumult –
wandering around here deceitfully.
He's a thief, if we allow it.
60 Watch out! Defend yourselves against him!'

The ostler roused up the whole crowd,
and it was a terrible tale.
They were scowling round about me,
64 nine at a time looking for me, all around me,
and I – terrible ugly bruises –
was keeping silent in the dark.
I prayed – not with a brave face –
68 in hiding, like a man afraid,
and by the power of precious, sincere prayer,
and by the grace of the true Jesus,
I reached – a knot of sleeplessness –
72 without reward, my own old bed.
I escaped – it is good the saints are near.
To God I pray for forgiveness.

Sarhau ei Was

Gŵyl Bedr y bûm yn edrych
Yn Rhosyr, lle aml gwŷr gwych,
Ar drwsiad pobl, aur drysor,
A gallu Môn gerllaw môr.
Yno'dd oedd, haul Wynedd yw,
Yn danrhwysg, Enid unrhyw,
Gwenddyn mynyglgrwn gwynddoeth,
A gwych oedd a gwiw a choeth,
Ac unsut, fy nyn geinsyw,
Yn y ffair â delw Fair fyw,
A'r byd, am ei gwynbryd gwiw,
Ar ei hôl, eiry ei heiliw.
Rhyfedd fu gan y lluoedd,
Rhodd o nef, y rhyw ddyn oedd.
Minnau o'm clwyf a'm anhun
Yn wylo byth yn ôl bun.
A fu was a fai faswach
Ei fryd didwyll a'i bwyll bach?
Ar gyfair y gofl ddiell,
Od gwn, y byddwn o bell,
Yny aeth, dyniolaeth dwys,
I loywlofft faen oleulwys.

Troes ugain i'm traws ogylch
O'm cyd-wtreswyr i'm cylch.
Prid i'r unben a'i chwennych,
Profais y gwin, prif was gwych;
Prynais, gwaith ni bu fodlawn,
Ar naid ddau alwynaid lawn.

Insulting his Servant

On St Peter's Day I was looking
in Rhosyr, a place full of fine folk,
at people's attire – golden treasure –
4 and the throng of Môn by the sea.
There she was – she is Gwynedd's sun –
like a blazing fire, another Enid,
a wise fair round-necked maid!
8 And she was gorgeous and fine and beautiful
and unique, my fine splendid girl
at the fair, the living image of Mary,
with the whole world, because of her fine fair face,
12 after her – the colour of snow.
It was a wonder to the crowds
– a gift from Heaven – the sort of girl she was.
And I, in my lovesickness and my sleeplessness,
16 always weeping after the girl.
Was there ever a lad who could be more useless,
sincere in his intent but with little sense?
With regard to that faultless armful,
20 to be sure, I stayed far away,
until she went – earnest her nature –
to a bright and fair upper room of stone.

A score of my fellow revellers
24 surrounded me on all sides.
Expensive for a lord who desires it,
I tried the wine – splendid first-rate lad.
I bought – a deed that was not fortunate –
28 at a single bound two full gallons.

Llys Rhosyr, gyda Llanbedr yn y pellter ✧
Rhosyr Court, with St Peter's Church in the distance

'Dos, was, o'r mygr gwmpas mau,
Dwg hyn i'r ferch deg gynnau.
Rhed hyd ei chlust a hustyng
I'w thwf tëyrnaidd, a thyng,
Mwyaf morwyn yng Ngwynedd
A garaf yw, 'm Gŵr a fedd.
Dyfydd hyd ei hystafell,
Dywaid, "Henffych, ddyn wych, well!"
Llym iawnrhwydd, "Llyma anrheg
I ti, yr addfwynddyn teg." '

'Pond cyffredin y dinas?
Paham na'th adwaenam, was?
Pell ynfyd yw, pwyll anfoes,
Pei rhôn, dywaid pwy a'i rhoes.'

'Dafydd, awenydd wiwnwyf,
Lwytu ŵr, a'i latai wyf.
Clod yng Ngwynedd a eddyw;
Clywwch ef; fal sain cloch yw.'

'Cyfodwch er pum harcholl!
A maeddwch ef! Mae'dd ywch oll?'

Dafydd:
'Go, boy, from these fine surroundings of mine.
Take this to the fair girl just now.
Run to her ear and whisper
32 to her majestic form, and swear
she is the maiden in Gwynedd
whom I love most, by the One who rules.
Go to her chamber,
36 say, "Greetings, splendid girl!"
keenly and fluently, "Here is a gift
for you, fair delightful girl." '

The girl:
'Isn't this a common town?
40 Why do I not know you, boy?
He is a fool from afar – uncouth judgement –
Nevertheless, tell me who gave it.'

The servant:
'Dafydd, poet of fine desire,
44 a dark grey man, and I am his messenger.
His fame has reached Gwynedd.
Listen to it. It is like the sound of a bell.'

The girl:
'Get up, by the five wounds!
48 And beat him! Where are you all?'

Cael y claerwin o'r dinas
A'i dywallt yng ngwallt fy ngwas.
Amarch oedd hynny ymy,
Amorth Mair i'm hoywgrair hy.
Os o brudd y'm gwarthruddiawdd
Yngod, cyfadnabod cawdd,
Asur a chadas gasul,
Eisiau gwin ar ei min mul!
Bei gwypwn, gwpl diletpai,
Madog Hir, fy myd, a'i câi.
Hwyr y'i gwnâi, hagr westai hy,
Einion Dot yn un diawty.
Hi a wŷl, bryd hoyw wylan,
Ei chlust â'i llygad achlân
Fyth weithion pan anfonwyf
I'r fun annyun o nwyf
Llonaid llwy o ddwfr llinagr
Yn anrheg, bid teg, bid hagr.

She took the fine wine from the town
And poured it in my lad's hair!
That was an insult to me,
52 *Mary's curse on my bold lively darling.*
If she seriously shamed me
there, acknowledging anger,
in her blue and caddice-trimmed cloak,
56 *may she lack wine on her foolish lips!*
If I had known – straight couple –
Madog Hir could have had her, my darling.
Reluctantly would – ugly bold guest –
60 *Einion Dot take her in any ale-house.*
She will see – face bright as a gull –
her own ear with her own eye
before I ever from now on send
64 *to a girl devoid of desire*
a spoonful of lukewarm water
as a gift, be she fair, be she foul.

Gwayw Serch

Y ferch yn yr aur llathrloyw
A welais, hoen geirwfais hoyw,
Yn aur o'r pen bwy gilydd,
Yn rhiain wiw, deuliw dydd,
Yn gwarando salm balchnoe
Yng nghôr Deinioel Bangor doe.

Love's Spear

I saw the girl in the bright shining gold
– brightness of lively rippling water –
in gold from head to toe,
4   a lovely damsel – the two colours of day –
listening to a song of Noah's ark
in the choir of Deiniol Bangor yesterday.

Cadeirlan Deiniol, Bangor ✧ *Cathedral Church of St Deiniol, Bangor*

Digon i'r byd o degwch;
Deugur, bryd Fflur, i'i brawd fflwch
Weled y wenferch wiwlwys,
Wi o'r dydd! mau wewyr dwys.
Â seithochr wayw y'm saethawdd
A sythdod, cymhendod cawdd;
Gwenwyn awch, gwn fy nychu,
Gwyn eiddigion gwlad Fôn fu.
Nis tyn dyn dan wybr sygnau,
I mewn y galon y mae.
Nis gorug gof ei guraw,
Nis gwnaeth llifedigaeth llaw,
Ni wŷs na lliw, gwiw gwawdradd,
Na llun y dost arf a'm lladd.
Gorwyf o'm gwiwnwyf a'm gwedd,
Gorffwyll am gannwyll Gwynedd.
Gwae fyfi, gwayw a'm hirbair
Gwyn fy myd, ail gwiwne Mair.
Gwydn ynof gwayw deunownych,
Gwas prudd a wnâi'r grudd yn grych.
Gwynia'n dost, gwenwyn a dâl,
Gwayw llifaid, gwäell ofal.
Esyllt bryd a'i dyd er dig,
Aseth cledr dwyfron ysig.
Trwm yw ynof ei hirgadw,
Trwyddew fy mron friwdon fradw,
Trefnloes fynawyd cariad,
Triawch saeth fydd brawdfaeth brad.

Enough beauty for the world;
8 *double pain – the face of Fflur – for her generous brother*
it was to see the beautiful fair girl, proper and lovely.
Alas the day! Serious pangs are mine.
With a seven-sided spear she pierced me,
12 *and stiffness – anger is suitable.*
Sharp poison – I know I'm growing weak –
was the wish of the jealous men of Môn.
No one under the heavenly signs can draw it out;
16 *it is inside my heart.*
No blacksmith beat it.
No hand whetted it.
Not known is the colour, worthy of praise,
20 *or the form of the cruel weapon that struck me.*
I have gone, from my usual vitality and my looks,
mad for the candle of Gwynedd.
Woe is me! She has long affected me with pain
24 *– I am blessed – a second fair-hued Mary.*
Firmly in me, a spear with eighteen pains
– a melancholy lad makes the cheek wrinkled –
hurts terribly, pays in poison,
28 *a sharp spear, a troublesome skewer.*
One with Esyllt's beauty placed it in anger,
thatching-rod of a wounded breast.
It is hard keeping it long within me,
32 *the auger in my bruised, broken breast,*
the painful condition of love's awl.
The triple-edged arrow is the foster-brother of betrayal.

Y Cloc

Cynnar fodd, cain arfeddyd,
Canu'dd wyf fi can hawdd fyd
I'r dref wiw ger Rhiw Rheon
Ar gwr y graig, a'r gaer gron.
Yno, gynt ei enw a gad,
Y mae dyn a'm adwaeniad.
Hawddamor heddiw yma
Hyd yn nhyddyn y dyn da.
Beunoeth, foneddigddoeth ferch,
Y mae honno i'm hannerch.

Bryd cwsg ym, a bradw y'i caid,
Breuddwyd yw, braidd y dywaid,
A'm pen ar y gobennydd,
Acw y daw cyn y dydd
Yng ngolwg, eang eilun,
Angel bach yng ngwely bun.
Tybiaswn o'm tyb isod
Gan fy mun gynnau fy mod.
Pell oedd rhyngof, cof a'i cais,
A'i hwyneb pan ddihunais.

Och i'r cloc yn ochr y clawdd
Du ei ffriw a'm deffroawdd.
Difwyn fo'i ben a'i dafod
A'i ddwy raff iddo a'i rod,
A'i bwysau, pellennau pŵl,
A'i fuarthau a'i forthwl,
A'i hwyaid yn tybiaid dydd,
A'i felinau aflonydd.
Cloc anfwyn mal clec ynfyd
Cobler brwysg, cabler ei bryd,
Cleddau eurych celwyddawg,
Cnecian ci yn cnocian cawg,
Mynychglap mewn mynachglos
Melin ŵyll yn malu nos.

The Clock

In a timely manner, with a fine purpose,
I am singing a hundred blessings
to the fine town near Rhiw Rheon
4 at the edge of the crag and the round fort.
There – of old her name was well-known –
is a girl who knew me.
Greetings here today
8 to the home of the worthy one.
Every night, wise noble girl,
she greets me.

As I sleep – and it was shattered –
12 there is a dream – it barely speaks –
with my head on the pillow.
There it comes, before day,
into view – a clear image:
16 a little angel in a maiden's bed.
I had imagined in my mind
that I was with my girl just then.
Far it was between me – memory seeks her –
20 and her face when I awoke.

Alas for the clock beside the dyke
 – black its look – which woke me up.
May its head and its tongue be useless,
24 and its two ropes, and its wheel,
and its weights – stupid balls –
and its frame, and its hammer,
and its ducks imagining it is day,
28 and its restless mills.
Rude clock like the foolish clack
of a drunken cobbler – curse its form –
the sword of a lying tinker,
32 a clattering dog banging a bowl,
the frequent clap, in the monks' cloister,
of a ghostly mill grinding at night.

Rhiw Rheon(?), Nant Rheon dan y coed ✧ *Rhiw Rheon(?), Nant Rheon under the trees*

A fu sadler, crwper crach,
Neu deiler anwadalach?
Oer ddilen ar ei ddolef
Am fy nwyn yma o nef.

Cael ydd oeddwn, coel ddiddos,
Hun o'r nef am hanner nos
Ym mhlygau hir freichiau hon,
Ymhlith Deifr ym mhleth dwyfron.
A welir mwy, alar maeth,
Wlad Eigr, ryw weledigaeth?

Was there ever a scabby-bottomed saddler
36 *or roof tiler more unstable?*
A miserable end to its clamour
for bringing me here from heaven!

I was getting – snug embrace –
40 *a heavenly sleep about midnight*
in the folds of her long arms,
amongst the English, lost in her breast.
Will more ever be seen – nourishing sorrow –
44 *– the land's Eigr – of such a vision?*

74

Eto rhed ati ar hynt,
Freuddwyd, ni'th ddwg afrwyddynt.
Gofyn i'r dyn dan aur do
A ddaw hun iddi heno
I roi golwg o'r galon,
Nith yr haul, unwaith ar hon.

Run to her again immediately,
Dream! It will not be a difficult journey for you.
Ask the girl beneath the golden canopy
48 *if sleep will come to her tonight*
to give a heartfelt vision,
niece of the sun, once more, of her.

Castell Aberhonddu, 'ger Rhiw Rheon' ◇ *Brecon Castle, 'near Rhiw Rheon'*

Y Dylluan

Truan i'r dylluan deg
Ar ddistial na rydd osteg:
Ni ad ym ganu 'mhader,
Ni thau tra fo siamplau sêr.
Ni chaf—och o'r gorafun!—
Gysgu, na heddychu, hun.

The Owl

It is sad that the fair owl
on a branch won't be quiet.
It doesn't allow me to sing my prayers,
4 *It won't be silent while there stars in the sky.*
I can not get – Oh, what a nuisance! –
to sleep or have any peace.

Y Dylluan, Llanllugan ✧ Owl, Llanllugan

Tŷ o drum yr ystlumod
A gais rhag piglaw ac ôd.
Beunoeth, bychan rhaib ynof,
I'm clustiau, ceiniogau cof,
Pan gaewyf, poen ogyfarch,
Fy llygaid, penaethiaid parch,
Hyn a'm deffry, ni hunais,
Cân y dylluan a'i llais,
A'i chrochwaedd aml a'i chrechwen
A'i ffals gywyddoliaeth o'i phen.
O hynny, modd yr hanwyf,
Hyd wawrddydd, annedwydd nwyf,
Canu bydd, annedwydd nâd,
'Hw ddy hw', hoyw ddyhead.

Ynni mawr, myn ŵyr Anna,
Annos cŵn y nos a wna.
Budrog yw, ddiwyw ddwywaedd,
Benfras, anghyweithas waedd;
Llydan dâl, griafal groth,
Llygodwraig hen llygadroth;
Ystig ddielwig eiliw,
Westn ei llys, ystaen ei lliw.

It is seeking shelter on the ridge of bats
8 against the piercing rain and snow.
Every night – little enchantment for me –
to my ears – memories pennies –
when I close – painful greeting –
12 my eyes – lords of respect –
this wakes me – I have not slept –
the song of the owl and its voice,
and its constant harsh cry and its screeching laugh,
16 and the false hymnody from its mouth.
From then on, as sure as I live,
until daybreak – miserable vigor –
it will be singing – miserable song –
20 'Hoo-the-hoo' – lively wheezing.

With great energy, by Anna's grandson,
it urges on the hounds of the night.
It's a slut, with its unfading double cry,
24 big-headed, with an unpleasant cry,
broad forehead, rowan-red belly,
old wide-eyed mouser,
unflagging, drab its appearance,
28 its court a rotten stump, its colour tin.

Uchel ei ffrec mewn decoed.
Och o'r cân uwch aerwy coed,
A'i gwedd, wynepryd dyn gwâr,
A'i sud, ellylles adar.
Pob edn, syfudr alltudryw,
A'i baedd. Ond rhyfedd ei byw?
Ffraethach yw hon mewn bronnallt
Y nos no'r eos o'r allt.
Ni thyn y dydd, crefydd craff,
Ei phen o geubren gobraff.
Udai'n ffraeth, adwen ei ffriw,
Edn i Wyn ap Nudd ydiw.
Ŵyll ffladr a gân i'r lladron,
Anffawd i'r tafawd a'r tôn!

Er tarfu y dylluan
Oddi wrthyf mae gennyf gân:
Rhof tra fwy'n aros y rhew
Oddaith ym mhob pren eiddew.

Loud its chatter throughout ten woods.
Oh! that song above the rows of trees,
and its appearance, with a gentle person's face,
32 *and its form, phantom of the birds.*
Every bird – dirty alien –
attacks it. Isn't it strange it's still alive?
It is more talkative on the hillside
36 *at night than the nightingale of the slope.*
In the daytime it does not poke – wise practice –
its head from a large hollow tree.
It was hooting constantly – I know its look!
40 *It is Gwyn ap Nudd's bird,*
a babbling wraith that sings for thieves.
Bad luck to its tongue and its tune!

To drive the owl away
44 *from me, I have a song:*
I will start, while I am waiting for the frost,
a blazing fire in every ivy-covered tree.

Y Bardd a'r Brawd Llwyd

Gwae fi na ŵyr y forwyn
Glodfrys, a'i llys yn y llwyn,
Ymddiddan y brawd llygliw
Amdanai y dydd heddiw.

    Mi a euthum at y Brawd
I gyffesu fy mhechawd.
Iddo 'dd addefais, od gwn,
Mae eilun prydydd oeddwn,
A'm bod erioed yn caru
Rhiain wynebwen aelddu,
Ac na bu ym o'm llawrudd
Les am unbennes na budd,
Ond ei charu'n hir wastad
A churio'n fawr o'i chariad,
A dwyn ei chlod drwy Gymru
A bod hebddi er hynny,
A damuno ei chlywed
I'm gwely rhof a'r pared.

    Heb y Brawd wrthyf yna,
'Mi a rown yt gyngor da.
O cheraist eiliw ewyn,
Lliw papir, oed hir hyd hyn,
Llaesa boen y dydd a ddaw,
Lles yw i'th enaid beidiaw,
A thewi â'r cywyddau
Ac arfer o'th baderau.
Nid er cywydd nac englyn
Y prynodd Duw enaid dyn.
Nid oes o'ch cerdd chwi, y glêr,
Ond truth a lleisiau ofer,
Ac annog gwŷr a gwragedd
I bechod ac anwiredd.
Nid da'r moliant corfforawl
A ddyco'r enaid i ddiawl.'

The Poet and the Grey Friar

Woe is me that the maiden of widespread fame,
with her court in the grove, does not know
of my conversation with the mouse-coloured friar
4 about her today.

I went to the friar
to confess my sin.
To him I admitted, indeed,
8 that I was a poor excuse for a poet,
and I had always loved
a fair-faced, black-browed young woman,
and that I had from my slayer no
12 benefit regarding that lady, nor favour,
only loving her long and constantly
and pining away greatly for love of her,
and carrying her fame throughout Wales,
16 and being without her in spite of that,
and wishing to feel her
in my bed between me and the wall.

The friar said to me then,
20 'I would give you good advice.
If you loved one the color of foam,
the colour of paper, for a long time till now,
ease the pain of the day that is coming
24 – It is good for your soul to stop –
and silence the cywyddau
and practice your prayers.
Not for a cywydd or an englyn
28 did God redeem man's soul.
There is nothing in your song, you poets,
but foolish talk and vain voices,
and inciting men and women
32 to sin and falsehood.
Not good is the praise of the flesh
which leads the soul to the devil.'

'A dwyn ei chlod drwy Gymru' (Aber Artro) ✧ *'And carrying her fame throughout Wales' (Mouth of the Artro)*

Minnau atebais i'r Brawd
Am bob gair ar a ddywawd.
'Nid ydyw Duw mor greulon
Ag y dywaid hen dynion.
Ni chyll Duw enaid gŵr mwyn
Er caru gwraig na morwyn.
Tripheth a gerir trwy'r byd:
Gwraig a hinon ac iechyd.
Merch sydd decaf blodeuyn
Yn y nef ond Duw ei hun.
O wraig y ganed pob dyn
O'r holl bobloedd ond tridyn.
Ac am hynny nid rhyfedd
Caru merched a gwragedd.

'O'r nef y cad pob digrifwch
Ac o uffern bob tristwch.
Cerdd a bair yn llawenach
Hen ac ieuanc, claf ac iach.
Cyn rheitied i mi brydu
Ag i tithau bregethu,
A chyn iawned ym glera
Ag i tithau gardota.
Pand englynion ac odlau
Yw'r hymner a'r segwensiau,
A chywyddau i Dduw lwyd
Yw llaswyr Dafydd Broffwyd?

'Nid â'r un bwyd ac enllyn
Y mae Duw'n porthi pob dyn.
Amser a osoded i fwyd
Ac amser i olochwyd,
Ac amser i bregethu
Ac amser i gyfaneddu.
Cerdd a genir ym mhob gwledd
I ddiddanu rhianedd,
A phader yn yr eglwys
I geisio tir Paradwys.

And I answered the friar
36 for every word that he said.
'God is not as cruel
as old men say.
God will not lose a gentle man's soul
40 for loving a wife or maiden.
Three things are loved throughout the world:
a woman and fair weather and health.
A maid is the fairest flower
44 in heaven except for God himself.
Everyone from all nations was born of woman
except for three people.
And therefore it is no wonder
48 that men love girls and women.

'From heaven came every joy
and from hell every sorrow.
Poetry makes happier
52 both old and young, sick and hale.
It is as fitting for me to make poetry
as for you to preach,
and as right for me to wander as a poet
56 as for you to beg.
Are not the hymnal and the sequences
englynion and awdlau,
and the psalter of the prophet David
60 cywyddau to holy God?

'God does not sustain everyone
with the same bread and butter.
A time was set for food
64 and a time for prayer
and a time to preach
and a time for entertaining.
Poems are sung at every feast
68 to delight young women,
and prayers in the church
to seek the land of Paradise.

'Gwir a ddywad Ystudfach
Gyda'i feirdd yn cyfeddach,
"Wyneb llawen llawn ei dŷ,
Wyneb trist drwg a ery."
Cyd caro rhai sancteiddrwydd
Eraill a gâr gyfanheddrwydd.
Anaml a ŵyr gywydd pêr
A phawb a ŵyr ei bader.
Ac am hynny, 'r deddfol Frawd,
Nid cerdd sydd fwyaf pechawd.

   'Pan fo cystal gan bob dyn
Glywed pader gan delyn
Â chan forynion Gwynedd
Glywed cywydd o faswedd
Mi a ganaf, myn fy llaw,
Y pader fyth heb beidiaw.
Hyd hynny mefl i Ddafydd
O chân bader, ond cywydd.'

'It is true what Ystudfach said
72 with his bards at a feast,
"A happy face, his house is full;
a sad face, evil awaits."
Though some may love sanctity,
76 others love entertainment.
Rare is someone who knows a sweet cywydd,
but everyone knows his prayers.
And therefore, devout friar,
80 it is not poetry that is the greatest sin.

When it will be as pleasing for everyone
to hear a prayer with a harp
as for the girls of Gwynedd
84 to hear a cywydd full of merriment,
I will sing, by my hand,
prayers forever without stopping.
Until then, shame on Dafydd
88 if he sings a prayer, rather than a cywydd.'

Noddwyr a Beirdd ✧ Patrons & Poets

'Gwenlloer Garawn' ✧ *'The fair moon of Caron'*

Merch o Is Aeron

Celennig yw cael annerch
Calon Is Aeron a'i serch.
Gwan y bardd sythardd, seithug,
Gwawn Geredigiawn a'i dug.

Gwae a fwrw, gwiw oferedd,
Ei serch, meirionesferch medd,
Llary bryd, hi yw lloer ei bro,
Lluniaeth ocr, lle ni thycio.
Gwae a wyl â gwyw olwg
Ar fun aur ddiaerfen wg,
Ni ddiddyr faint ei ddeuddeigr
O'i chariad, diwygiad Eigr.
Gwae a oerddeily gwayw erddi
Oddi fewn, mal ydd wyf i,
Yn drysor bun, yn drasyth,
Yn ddadl fawr, yn ddidal fyth.
Gwae a wnêl rhag rhyfel rhew
Dŷ ar draeth, daear drathew,
Bydd anniogel wely,
Byr y trig a'r berw a'i try.
Gwae a gâr, gwiw y gorwyf,
Gwen drais, gwenifiais gwayw nwyf,
Gwynllathr ei gwedd, gweunllethr gwawn,
Gwynlliw'r geirw, gwenlloer Garawn.

Erfai leddf, oerfel iddi,
Ar fy hoen neur orfu hi.
Eirian liw, oroen lawir,
Euren deg o Aeron dir,
Aerau len, eiry oleuni,
Ar ei hyd a eura hi.

A Girl from Is Aeron

It's a New Year's gift, getting a greeting
from the heart of Is Aeron and its love.
Weak is the handsome, upright bard, useless.
4 The gossamer of Ceredigion has taken him.

Woe to one who bestows – fitting folly –
his love – mistress of mead,
gentle countenance, she is her region's moon –
8 where it will not thrive – it's a form of usury.
Woe to one who looks with a wan gaze
on the frown of a golden maid slow to anger.
She doesn't care how copious are his tears
12 from loving her, more beautiful than Eigr.
Woe to one who sadly suffers on her account
a sharp pain within, as I do
– a treasure of a maid, upright –
16 in a great complaint, forever unrequited.
Woe to one who builds, in the war against cold,
a house on the shore, soil too thick;
it will be a perilous bed;
20 briefly will it remain and the foam will overturn it.
Woe to one who loves – I have done right,
(a fair one's tyranny), I've served a sharp desire;
bright and beautiful her face, moor's gossamer,
24 pure hue of the waves – the fair moon of Caron.

Faultless gentle one – coldness to her –
she has overcome my joy!
Fair of hue, generous countenance,
28 fair golden dear from the land of Aeron,
banner of battles, brightness of snow,
she gilds it from one end to the other.

Marwnad Rhydderch ab Ieuan Llwyd

Doe clywais, neur geisiais gêl,
Dair och ar lethrdir uchel.
Ni meddyliwn, gwn gannoch,
Y rhôi ŵr fyth y rhyw och.
Ni bu i'm gwlad, rhoddiad rhydd,
Na llif cwyn, na llef cynydd,
Na meingorn ar lethr mangoed,
Na chloch uwch no'r och a roed.

Pa dwrw yw hwn, pedeiroch?
Pefr loes, pwy a roes yr och?
Llywelyn, o'r syddyn serch,
A roddes hon am Rydderch,
Fychan, garllaw ei lân lys,
Ffyddfrawd Rhydderch ddiffoddfrys.
Och Amlyn o'i dyddyn dig,
Alaeth mamaeth, am Emig;
Och gŵr a fai'n awch garu
Ei gâr, o fawr alar fu;
A'r drydedd och, gloch y Glyn,
Llef ail, a roes Llywelyn.

Pan gaewyd, saith guddiwyd serch,
Gwin rhoddiad, genau Rhydderch,
Darfu, gwn y'm dierfir,
Ben Deheubarth wen yn wir.
Darfu'r foes dirfawr o fedd,
Darfu daearu dewredd.
Gorwyn alarch yng ngwarchae,
Gorwedd mewn maenfedd y mae.
Natur boen, nid hwy yw'r bedd,
Syth drudfalch, no saith droedfedd.

Lament for Rhydderch ab Ieuan

Yesterday I heard – I sought shelter –
three cries on a high hillside.
I wouldn't have thought – I know a hundred cries –
a man could ever give such a cry.
There was never in my land – generous benefactor –
either flood of grief or huntsman's yell,
either shrill horn on a wooded slope,
or bell louder than the cry that was given.

What noise is this – four cries,
pure agony – who gave that cry?
Llywelyn, from the home of love,
gave it for Rhydderch,
Fychan, beside his fair court,
faithful friend of Rhydderch, dead too soon.
The cry of Amlyn from his house of grief
– a foster-mother's sorrow – for Amig,
the cry of a man who keenly loved
his kinsman, it was from great sorrow.
And the third cry – bell of the Glyn –
an equal yell, Llywelyn gave.

When Rhydderch's lips – giver of wine –
were closed – love was hidden seven times over –
at an end – I know I am disarmed –
was the head of fair Deheubarth truly.
At an end was the custom of abundant mead-giving.
At an end was burying bravery.
A brilliant white swan confined,
he rests in a stone grave.
A painful state, the grave is no longer
– straight, harsh, pitiless – than seven feet.

Pregeth ryfedd oedd weddu
Dan hyn o dywerchyn du,
Gwybodau, synhwyrau serch,
Gwmpas rodd gampus Rydderch,
A'i wiwdawd digollwawd gall,
A'i gryfgorff gwyn digrifgall,
A'i gampau, chwedl doniau dawn,
A'i lwyddiant a'i oleuddawn,
A'i ras, gyweithas ieithydd,
A'i glod, och ddyfod ei ddydd!

Trwst oedd oer trist ddaearu,
Trugarog o farchog fu.
Trugaredd, ddisymlwedd serch,
A roddo Duw i Rydderch.

A strange lesson was yoking
32 *under such black sod as this*
the knowledge, the sense of love,
the full scope of Rhydderch's excellent gift,
and his wise, praiseworthy splendour,
36 *and his pleasingly wise, fair, strong body,*
and his feats – a tale of natural gifts of genius –
and his success and his bright genius,
and his grace, genial speaker,
40 *and his fame. Alas! that his day has come!*

A great noise was the cold, sad burial.
He was a merciful knight.
May God show mercy
44 *–love's gentle form – to Rhydderch.*

Moliant Llywelyn ap Gwilym

Llyfr dwned Dyfed, dyfyn—ar windai
    I randir Llywelyn;
      Llannerch, aed annerch pob dyn,
      Lle twymlys llu, at Emlyn.   4

Llyn i barc Emlyn, camlas—hyd Deifi,
    A'r tefyrn ymhob plas,
      Lluddied gardd, lladded ei gas,
      Lle bo'r orddod, llwybr urddas.   8

Llwybr urddas, bar bras yn bwrw bryn,—eglur
    Oglais Lloegr a Phrydyn,
      Lle dêl yr holl fyd a dynn,
      Llaw hael, ac enw Llywelyn.   12

Praise of Llywelyn ap Gwilym

Dyfed's grammar book summons to wine-cellars
    in Llywelyn's territory.
      An oasis, let a greeting go to everyone,
      a warm court for a host, at Emlyn.

A lake for Emlyn's park, a channel to the Teifi
    and taverns every place.
      Let him prevent shame, let him strike his enemy;
      where the blow may be is a pathway of honour.

A pathway of honour, a thick spear striking the mighty,
    a clear provocation to England and Scotland,
      wherever he comes, the whole world draws near,
      a generous hand, and the name of Llywelyn.

Adfail Castellnewydd Emlyn ✧ *Ruins of the castle at Newcastle Emlyn*

'Lle beirw Teifi' ger Castell Newydd Emlyn ✧ 'Where Teifi roils' near Newscastle Emlyn

Llywelyn a'u myn ym ynni—a grym,
    Llawenfab Gwilym, erddrym wrddri,
Llai ymadrawdd cawdd i'n coddi—no chaeth,
    Llywodraeth a wnaeth a maeth i mi.
Llafuriawdd, berthawdd i borthi—digeirdd,
    Llys ym mryn y beirdd, lle heirdd yw hi,
Lle gnawd cael gwasgawd a gwisgi—ddillad,
    Llety anghaead, wastad westi.
Lle cynefin gwin a gweini—heilgyrn,
    Lle chwyrn, llwybr tefyrn, lle beirw Teifi.

Llywelyn wishes for me vigour and strength,
    the joyful son of Gwilym, noble mighty ruler.
With fewer angry words to anger us than a serf,
    he governed and nurtured me.
He built and adorned to sustain the renowned
    a court on the poets' hill. It is a place of beauties,
a place where receiving shelter and fine clothing is usual,
    an open lodging, with a constant welcome.
A customary place for wine and serving drinking horns,
    a lively place, taverns' path, where Teifi roils.

16

20

Lle dichwerw, aserw, o erysi—bryd,
  Lle chwery esbyd byd heb oedi.
Lle maith yn llawnwaith llenwi—buelin,
  Lle mae ufuddwin llym i feddwi.
Lle o'th nerth, Dduw ferth, ydd af fi—drachefn,
  Lle anarlloestrefn, llanw aur llestri.
Llys eurwr, a'i gwnaeth llu seiri—yn falch,
  Lliwgaer yn lasgalch, llugyrn losgi.
Llawnaf, dianaf, daioni—mynud,
  Lluniaeth ffraeth, ffrwythdud, glud glodfori.
Llwybreiddwlad, gariad Gwri—Wallt Euryn,
  Llywelyn drawstyn a â drosti.
Llywiawdr, ymerawdr meiri—Edelffled,
  Llyw yw ar Ddyfed, llawer ddofi.
Llorf llwyth, ei dylwyth hyd Wyli—y traidd,
  Llariaidd, brawdwriaidd, ail Bryderi.
Llathrlaw ysb euraw, ysberi—gwëyll,
  Llid Pyll, arf dridryll, arfod Rodri.
Llinongadr, baladr Beli—yng nghyngaws,
  Llwyrnaws Llŷr hoywdraws, llew wrhydri.
Llawen grair, a'n pair yn peri—llwyddfoes,
  Llawenydd a roes am oes i mi.
Llywelyn derwyn i dorri—aergad,
  Llawfad aur-rhuddiad a ŵyr rhoddi.
Llwydda, na threia, Un a Thri—rhag llaw,
  Llwyddaw dawn iddaw, Duw i'w noddi.

24
A place not bitter, bright, of a wondrous aspect,
  where the world's guests play without delay.
A large place filled with the work of filling horns,
  where there is strong wine ready for getting drunk.
Where by thy strength, glorious God, I shall return,
28
  a place of not empty rooms, filling golden vessels.
A fine man's court, a host of carpenters made it proudly,
  a colourful, whitewashed fort, lanterns burning.
Fullest, faultless, courteous goodness,
32
  ready provisions, fruitful land, constant praising.
Orderly country, the love of Gwri Golden Hair,
  mighty Llywelyn rules over it.
Ruler, emperor over Aethelfrith's officers,
36
  he is helmsman of Dyfed, taming many.
Pillar of the people, his kin extend as far as Gwili,
  kind-hearted, judicial, a second Pryderi.
A bright hand with gold for guests, spears splintered,
40
  Pyll's anger, weapon in pieces, the blow of Rhodri.
Strong ash spear of Beli in battle,
  all the qualities of noble, mighty Llŷr, a brave lion.
A joyful treasure, who brings to us prosperity,
44
  he has given me joy for all my life.
Llywelyn, eager to crush a battalion,
  red-gold's good hand who knows how to give.
Promote, do not diminish, him, Three-in-One, henceforth,
48
  increase his talents. God protect him.

Cywydd Mawl i Ifor Hael

Ifor, aur o faerwriaeth
Deg yw'r fau, diegr o faeth.
Dewraf wyd ac euraf gŵr
Dy ddilyn, dieiddilwr:
Myned o'm gwlad, dyfiad iôr,
Â'th glod, a dyfod, Ifor.
Myfi yw, ffraethlyw ffrwythlawn,
Maer dy dda, mawr yw dy ddawn.

Ys dewr, ystyriol ydwyd,
Ystôr ym, ys da ŵr wyd.
Telais yt wawd tafawd hoyw,
Telaist ym fragod duloyw.
Rhoist ym swllt, rhyw ystum serch,
Rhoddaf yt brifenw Rhydderch.
Cyfarf arf, eirf ni'th weheirdd,
Cyfaillt a mab aillt y beirdd,
Cadarn wawr, cedyrn wiwryw,
Caeth y glêr, cywaethog lyw.
Da wyd a syberw dy ach,
Duw a fedd, dau ufuddach
Wyd i'th fardd, pellgardd pwyllgall,
Llywiwr llu, no'r llaw i'r llall.

In Praise of Ifor Hael

Ifor, a splendid fair stewardship
is mine, no sour nurturing.
You are the bravest and most splendid man
4 *to follow, no weakling.*
I go from my land, lord of full stature,
with your fame, and return, Ifor.
I am, fruitful powerful lord,
8 *steward of your goods. Great are your virtues.*

You are brave, thoughtful,
a treasure for me. You are a good man.
I paid elegant songs of praise to you,
12 *you paid bright black bragget to me.*
You gave me a shilling, a sign of love,
I give you Rhydderch's epithet.
Well-armed warrior, arms do not impede you,
16 *friend and bondman of bards,*
a strong chieftain of strong men's stock,
slave of poets, wealthy lord.
You are good and your line proud.
20 *By God who rules, twice as faithful*
are you to your bard, far from shame, wise, discerning,
leader of a host, as one hand is to the other.

O'm iaith y rhylunieithir,
Air nid gwael, arnad y gwir.
O'm pen fy hun, pen cun cyrdd,
Y'th genmyl wyth ugeinmyrdd.
Hyd yr ymddaith dyn eithaf,
Hyd y try, hwyl hy, haul haf,
Hyd yr hëir y gwenith,
A hyd y gwlych hoywdo gwlith,
Hyd y sych gwynt, hynt hyntiaw,
A hyd y gwlych hoywdeg law,
Hyd y gwŷl golwg digust,
Hydr yw, a hyd y clyw clust,
Hyd y mae iaith Gymräeg,
A hyd y tyf hadau teg,
Hardd Ifor, hoywryw ddefod,
Hir dy gledd, hëir dy glod.

Through my language is set out
– no mean word – the truth about you.
Through my own mouth, chief lord of multitudes,
eight score hosts praise you.
As far as anyone's farthest journey,
as far, bold course, as the summer sun turns,
as far as wheat is sown,
and as far as the excellent covering of dew wets,
as far as the wind dries, following its path,
and as far as the excellent fair rain wets,
as far as unobscured vision sees,
– it is powerful – and as far as ear hears,
as far as there is the Welsh language,
as far as fair seeds grow,
beautiful Ifor – excellent custom,
long your sword – is your fame sown.

Basaleg

Cerdda was, câr ddewiswyrdd,
Ceinfyd gwymp, is caenfedw gwyrdd;
O Forgannwg dwg ddydd da
I Wynedd, heilfedd hwylfa,
Ac annwyl wyf, befrnwyf byd,
Ac annerch wlad Fôn gennyd.
Dywaid, i'm gwlad ni'm gadwyd,
Duw a'i gŵyr, dieuog wyd,
Fy mod es talm, salm Selyf,

Basaleg, Ifor Hael's Home

Go, lad, enjoy the fine greenery,
the fine fair world, under the green birch canopy.
From Morgannwg take 'Good day'
to Gwynedd, mead-strewn path,
– and I am beloved, the world's bright feeling –
and greet the land of Môn.
Say – I'm not allowed in my own land;
God knows, you are not at fault –
that I for some time – psalm of Solomon –

Adfail Gwernyclepa, tŷ Ifor Hael ger Basaleg ✧ *Ruins of Gwernyclepa, home of Ifor Hael near Basaleg*

Yn caru dyn uwch Caerdyf.
Nid salw na cham fy namwain,
Nid serch ar finrhasglferch fain,
Mawrserch Ifor a'm goryw,
Mwy no serch ar ordderch yw.
Serch Ifor a glodforais,
Nid fal serch anwydful Sais,
Ac nid af, perffeithiaf pôr,
Os eirch ef, o serch Ifor,
Nac undydd i drefydd drwg,
Nac unnos o Forgannwg.
Pand digrif yng ngŵydd nifer
Caru, claernod saethu, clêr?

Goludog hebog hybarch,
Gŵr ffyrf iawn ei gorff ar farch.
Gŵr yw o hil goreuwawr,
Gwiw blaid, helm euraid, hael mawr;
Cwympwr aer cyflymdaer coeth,
Cwmpasddadl walch campusddoeth;
Carw difarw, Deifr ni oddef,
Cywir iawn y câi wyr ef;
Ufudd a da ei ofeg,
Ofer dyn wrth Ifor deg.

Mawr anrhydedd a'm deddyw:
Mi a gaf, o byddaf byw,
Hely â chwn, nid haelach iôr,
Ac yfed gydag Ifor,
A saethu rhygeirw sythynt
A bwrw gweilch i wybr a gwynt,
A cherddau tafodau teg
A solas ym Masaleg;
Gware ffristiawl a thawlbwrdd
Yn un gyflwr â'r gŵr gwrdd.

have loved one above Cardiff.
Neither shabby nor unworthy is my fortune.
12 *Not the love of a slender, smooth-lipped maiden –*
a great love for Ifor has overwhelmed me.
It is greater than love for a mistress.
I have praised the love of Ifor,
16 *not like the love of a fool of an Englishman,*
and I will not go – most perfect lord –
if he asks, because of love of Ifor,
even a single day to wicked towns,
20 *nor a single night from Morgannwg.*
Is it not pleasant in the presence of a host
to love poets who shoot at a clear target?

A revered and wealthy hawk,
24 *a well-built man upon a horse.*
He is a man descended from the finest lord,
a splendid company, gold-helmed, very generous.
Overthrower of an army, swift, eager, refined,
28 *all-encompassing in debate, a wise, clever hawk.*
An undying stag, he does not abide the English.
Men would find him very true.
His intention faithful and good,
32 *any man is worthless compared to fair Ifor.*

Great honour has happened to me:
I shall have, if I live,
hunting with hounds – no more generous lord –
36 *and drinking with Ifor*
and shooting at fine, straight-running deer
and casting hawks to the sky and wind
and songs from fair tongues
40 *and solace at Basaleg,*
playing ffristial *and* tawlbwrdd
as an equal with that valiant man.

O châi neb, cytundeb coeth,
Rhagor rhag y llall rhygoeth,
Rhugl â cherdd y'i anrhegaf,
Rhagor rhag Ifor a gaf.
Nid hael wrth gael ei gyfryw,
Nid dewr neb; band tëyrn yw?
Nid af o'i lys, diful iôr,
Nid ufudd neb ond Ifor.

If one gets – complete concord –
the better of the excellent other,
I shall reward him with an eloquent song.
I shall get the better of Ifor.
No generous one is his like,
no one as brave. Is he not a king?
I shall not leave his court – bold lord.
No one is faithful but Ifor.

44

48

Diolch am Fenig

Ifor ydoedd afradaur,
O'i lys nid âi bys heb aur.
Doe yr oeddwn ar giniaw
I'w lys yn cael gwin o'i law.
Mi a dyngaf â'm tafawd,
Ffordd y try dydd, gwëydd gwawd:
Gorau gwraig hyd ar Geri
A gorau gŵr yw d'ŵr di.
Tra fu'n trafaelu trwy fodd,
Trwy foliant y trafaelodd.

Y dydd y doethum o'i dai
â'i fenig dwbl o fwnai,
Benthig ei fenig i'w fardd
A roes Ifor resawfardd.
Menig gwynion tewion teg
A mwnai ym mhob maneg:
Aur yn y naill, dyaill dau,
Arwydd oedd, o'r llaw orau,
Ac ariant, moliant milioedd,
O fewn y llall, f'ynnill oedd.
Merched a fydd yn erchi
Benthig fy menig i mi.
Ni roddaf, dygaf yn deg,
Rodd Ifor rwydd ei ofeg.
Ni chaiff merch, er eu herchi,
Mwy no gŵr, fy menig i.
Ni wisgaf fenig nigus
O groen mollt i grino 'mys.
Gwisgaf, ni fynnaf ei fâr,
Hyddgen y gŵr gwahoddgar,
Menig gŵyl am fy nwylaw,
Ni bydd mynych y'u gwlych glaw.

Thanking Ifor Hael for Gloves

Ifor was lavish with gold.
Not a finger would leave his court without gold.
Yesterday I was at dinner
4   *in his court getting wine from his hand.*
I swear with my tongue,
as the day turns – weaver of praise –
best wife as far as Ceri,
8   *and your husband is the best man.*
While he was travelling as he wished,
he travelled with praise.

The day I left his court
12 *with his gloves doubly filled with money,*
Ifor the poet-welcomer
lent his gloves to his poet.
Fine, thick, white gloves
16 *with money in each glove:*
gold in the one – he possesses two,
it was a sign – from the best hand,
and silver – the praise of thousands –
20 *in the other – it was my reward.*
Girls will be asking
to borrow my gloves from me.
I shall not give – I will keep fairly –
24 *Ifor's gift – bountiful is his intent.*
No girl shall get, despite asking for them,
any more than a man, my gloves!
I shall not wear cheap gloves
28 *of ram skin to wrinkle my finger.*
I shall wear – I do not wish for his anger –
the buckskin of the hospitable man,
festive gloves for my hands.
32 *Not often will the rain wet them.*

Y Wennallt ✧ *The Wennallt*

Rhoddaf i hwn, gwn ei ged,
O nawdd rugl neuadd Reged,
Bendith Taliesin wingost
A bery byth heb air bost.
Ar ben y bwrdd erbyn bwyd
Yno'r êl yn yr aelwyd,
Lle trosaf ran o'm annerch,
Lle dewr mab, lle diwair merch,

I will give him – I know his favour,
from the fluent patronage of Rheged's hall –
the blessing of wine-giving Taliesin
36 *which will last forever without a word of boast.*
At the head of the table before dinner,
may it go there, on his hearth,
the place I will direct part of my greeting,
40 *place of brave lads, place of chaste maidens,*

Lle trig y bendefigaeth,
Yn wleddau, 'n foethau, yn faeth,
Yn wragedd teg eu hegin,
Yn weilch, yn filgwn, yn win,
Yn ysgarlad, rhad rhydeg,
Yn aur tawdd, yn eiriau teg.
Nid oes bren yn y Wennallt
Na bo'n wyrdd ei ben a'i wallt,
A'i gangau yn ogyngerth
A'i ŵn a'i bais yn un berth.
Ponid digrif i brifardd
Gweled, hoyw gynired hardd,
Arglwyddïaeth dugiaeth deg
A seiliwyd ym Masaleg?

Menig o'i dref a gefais,
Nid fal menig Seisnig Sais,
Menig, pur galennig, pôr,
Mwyn gyfoeth, menig Ifor.
Fy mendith wedi'i nithiaw
I dai Ifor Hael y daw.

place where lordship resides,
in feasts, in luxury, in sustenance,
in women with fair offspring,
44 *in hawks, in hounds, in wine,*
in scarlet – splendid bounty –
in pure gold, in fair words.
There is no tree in the Wennallt
48 *that does not have a head and hair of green,*
and its branches closely woven
and its gown and its tunic forming a single copse.
Is it not pleasant for a master-poet
52 *to see – lively, lovely concourse –*
the lordship of a fair dukedom
established at Basaleg?

I have had gloves from his residence,
56 *not like some Englishman's English gloves,*
gloves – pure gift – of a lord,
noble riches, Ifor's gloves.
My winnowed blessing
60 *will come to the court of Ifor Hael.*

Marwnad Gruffudd Gryg

Tost oedd ddwyn, trais cynhwynawl,
Tlws o'n mysg, Taliesin mawl.
Tristeais, nid trais diarw,
Trwm, oer, fal y trywyr marw.
Treiwyd gwawd, nid rhaid gwadu,
Tros fyd, gwladeiddiaf trais fu.
Tros fy ngran, ledchwelan lif,
Try deigr am ŵr tra digrif.

Lament for Gruffudd Gryg

It was cruel taking – inherent violence –
a jewel from our midst, the Taliesin of praise.
I mourned – no gentle violence –
heavily, coldly, as for the three dead men.   4
Poetry has been diminished, no need to deny it,
across the world. It was the crudest violence.
Across my cheek – foolish flood –
roll tears for a most delightful man.   8

Llan-faes, yn edrych tuag at y Carneddau ✧ *Fryars Bay, Llan-faes, looking towards the Carneddau peaks*

Gruffudd, huawdl ei awdlef,
Gryg ddoeth, myn y grog, oedd ef.
Ys dig am ei ostegion,
Ysgwîr mawl, eos gwŷr Môn,
Lluniad pob dyall uniawn
A llyfr cyfraith yr iaith iawn,
Agwyddor y rhai gwiwddoeth
A ffynnon cerdd a'i phen coeth,
A'i chyweirgorn, ddiorn dda,
A'i chyweirdant, och wyrda!
Pwy a gân ar ei lân lyfr,
Prydydd Goleuddydd liwddyfr?
Parod o'i ben awengerdd,
Primas ac urddas y gerdd.

Ni chair sôn gair o gariad,
Ni chân neb, gwn ochain, nâd,
Er pan aeth, alaeth olud,
I dan fedd i dewi'n fud.
Ni chwardd udfardd o adfyd,
Ni bu ddigrifwch o'r byd.
Ni bu edn glân a ganai,
Nid balch ceiliog mwyalch Mai.
Ni chynnydd mewn serch annog,
Ni chân nac eos na chog,
Na bronfraith ddwbliaith ddiblyg
Ni bydd gwedy Gruffudd Gryg,
Na chywydd dolydd na dail,
Na cherddi, yn iach irddail!

Tost o chwedl gan fun edlaes
Roi 'nghôr llawn fynor Llan-faes
Gimin, dioer, gem a'n deiryd,
O gerdd ag a roed i gyd.
Rhoed serchowgrwydd agwyddor
I mewn cist ym min y côr.
Cist o dderw, cystudd irad,
A gudd gwalch y gerdd falch fad;

Wise Gruffudd – eloquent his fine poetry –
Gryg it was, by the Cross.
There is grief for his poems,
12   square of praise, nightingale of the men of Môn,
limner of all true understanding,
and law book of proper language,
alphabet of the worthy and wise,
16   and wellspring of song and its refined head,
and its tuning key, faultless and good,
and its keynote string. Alas, noblemen!
Who will sing from his pure book,
20   the poet of Goleuddydd of the colour of water?
Readily from his mouth came inspired song,
the primate and nobility of song.

There is no mention of a word of love,
24   no one sings – I know sighing – a song
since he went – abundance of sorrow –
into the grave to become silent and mute.
No howling poet laughs, for wretchedness.
28   No joy was in the world.
No pure bird would sing.
Not proud, the blackbird of May.
No increase in love's urging.
32   No nightingale or cuckoo sings,
no unswerving double-tongued thrush.
There will be after Gruffudd Gryg,
no cywydd of meadows or leaves,
36   nor songs. Farewell, green leaves!

Bitter news for a mournful maid,
placing in the marble-filled chancel of Llan-faes
as much – God knows, a jewel that was ours –
40   song as was placed there altogether.
The alphabet of loving was placed
in a coffin at the edge of the chancel.
A chest of oak – bitter grief –
44   hides the hawk of fair proud song.

O gerddi swllt, agwrdd sâl,
Ni chaid un gistiaid gystal.
O gerdd euraid gerddwriaeth
Dôi'i rym i gyd yn derm gaeth.
Llywiwr iawngamp llariangerdd,
Llyna gist yn llawn o gerdd!
Och haelgrair Dduw Uchelgrist,
Na bai a egorai'r gist!

O charai ddyn wych eirian
Gan dant glywed moliant glân,
Gweddw y barnaf gerdd dafawd,
Ac weithian gwan ydiw'n gwawd.
Ef aeth y brydyddiaeth deg
Mal ar wystl, mul yw'r osteg.
Gwawd graffaf gwedy Gruffudd
Gwaethwaeth heb ofyddiaeth fydd.

Edn glwys ei baradwyslef,
Ederyn oedd o dir nef.
O nef y doeth, goeth gethlydd,
I brydu gwawd i bryd gwŷdd;
Awenfardd a fu winfaeth,
I nef, gwiw oedd ef, ydd aeth.

Of songs for a treasured one – great reward –
there has never been as fine a chestful.
From the art of poetry's golden song,
48 *all his strength has come to a confining end.*
Excellent ruler of gentle song,
behold there a chest full of song!
Alas, holy generous God, Christ on high,
52 *that there was no one who could open that coffin.*

If a bright, excellent girl ever loved
to hear pure praise with harp-strings,
I declare that poetry is widowed,
56 *and now our praise is feeble.*
It is as if fair poetry has been
taken hostage. Sad is the silence.
After Gruffudd the strongest praise
60 *will get worse and worse without Ovid's art.*

A bird, with his beautiful voice of paradise,
he was a bird from the land of heaven.
From heaven he came, a pure song-bird,
64 *to praise in verse the beauty of the woods.*
He was an inspired poet, wine-nourished.
He went – he was worthy – to heaven.

'ac ni chanaf mwy' ✧ 'and I shall sing no more'

Adfail Brogynin, tŷ Dafydd, 2017 ✧ *The ruins of Brogynin, Dafydd's home, 2017*

Yr Adfail

'Tydi, y bwth tinrhwth twn
Rhwng y gweundir a'r gwyndwn,
Gwae a'th weles, dygesynt,
Yn gyfannedd gyntedd gynt,
Ac a'th wŷl heddiw'n friw frig,
Dan dy ais yn dŷ ysig.
A hefyd ger dy hoywfur
Ef a fu ddydd, cerydd cur,
Ynod ydd oedd ddiddanach
Nog yr wyd, y gronglwyd grach,
Pan welais, pefr gludais glod,
Yn dy gongl, un deg yngod,
Forwyn, foneddigfwyn fu,
Hoywdwf yn ymgyhydu,
A braich pob un, cof un fydd,
Yn gwlm amgylch ei gilydd:
Braich meinir, briw awch manod,
Goris clust goreuwas clod,
A'm braich innau, somau syml,
Dan glust asw dyn glwys disyml.
Hawddfyd gan fasw i'th fraswydd,
A heddiw nid ydiw'r dydd'.

'Ys mau gŵyn, gwirswyn gwersyllt,
Am hynt a wnaeth y gwynt gwyllt.
Ystorm o fynwes dwyrain
A wnaeth cur hyd y mur main.
Uchenaid gwynt, gerrynt gawdd,
Y deau a'm didyawdd'.

The Ruin

'You, broken-down shack with a gaping backside,
between the moorland and the fallow,
Woe to any who saw you – they would think –
4   as a delightful hall of old,
and who see you today with a shattered roof,
beneath your ribs a broken house.
And moreover, by your fine wall
8   there was a day – painful rebuke –
within you that it was more joyful
than you are now, wretched framework,
when I saw – brilliantly I spread her fame –
12   in your corner – a fair one within –
a maiden – she was noble and genteel –
finely shaped, lying beside me,
with each one's arm – her memory shall remain –
16   entwined around the other:
a graceful girl's arm, bright as fine snow,
beneath the ear of the best lad for praise,
and my own arm – simple tricks –
20   under the left ear of a beautiful, gentle girl.
A happy time for the joyful under your thick beams,
but today is not that day.'

The Ruin:
'My complaint – truly the spell of a host –
24   is about the path of the wild wind.
A storm from the bosom of the east
beat along the stone wall.
The moan of the wind – path of anger –
28   from the south ruined me.'

'Ai'r gwynt a wnaeth helynt hwyr?
Da nithiodd dy do neithwyr.
Hagr y torres dy esyth.
Hudol enbyd yw'r byd byth.
Dy gongl, mau ddeongl ddwyoch,
Gwely ym oedd, nid gwâl moch.
Doe'r oeddud mewn gradd addwyn
Yn glyd uwchben fy myd mwyn.
Hawdd o ddadl, heddiw 'dd ydwyd,
Myn Pedr, heb na chledr na chlwyd.
Amryw bwnc ymwnc amwyll.
Ai hwn yw'r bwth twn bath twyll?'

'Aeth talm o waith y teulu,
Dafydd, â chroes. Da foes fu.'

Dafydd:
'Is it the wind that caused this trouble of late?
It winnowed your roof well last night.
It horribly damaged your thatching-laths.

32 *The world is always dangerously deceptive.*
Your corner – two cries of realization are mine –
was a bed for me, not a pigsty.
Yesterday you were in a fine condition,

36 *snug over my gentle dear.*
Easy to argue, today you are,
by Peter, without rafter or roofing.
Many an event causes sudden madness.

40 *Is this broken-down shack some sort of illusion?'*

The Ruin:
'A great deal of the household's work has gone,
Dafydd, to the grave. It was a good way of life.'

Y Drindod

Da fu'r Drindod heb dlodi
A wnaeth nef a byd i ni.
Da fu'r Tad yn anad neb
Roi Anna ddiwair wyneb.
Da fu Anna dwf uniawn
Ddwyn Mair Forwyn ddinam iawn.
Da fu Fair ddiwair eiriawl
Ddwyn Duw i ddiwyno diawl.
Da fu Dduw Iôr, ddioer oroen,
Â'i Groes ddwyn pumoes o'u poen.
Da y gwnêl Mab Mair, air addef,
Ein dwyn oll bob dyn i nef.

The Trinity

Good was the Trinity without stint
who made heaven and earth for us.
Good was the Father above anyone,
for giving us Anna, of pure honour.
Good was Anna, of upright form,
for bearing the immaculate Virgin Mary.
Good was Mary, of pure intercession,
for bearing God to destroy the devil.
Good was the Lord God – certain joy –
with his Cross for bearing the five ages from their pain.
Good may the Son of Mary do
bearing us all, every one, to heaven.

4

8

12

Y Drindod a'r mab Iesu ✧ *The Trinity and the Christ child*
Llanrhychwyn

104

Edifeirwch

Prid o swydd, prydais iddi,
Prydydd i Forfudd wyf i.
Myn y Gŵr a fedd heddiw,
Mae gwayw i'm pen am wen wiw
Ac i'm tâl mae gofalglwyf.
Am aur o ddyn marw ydd wyf.

Pan ddêl i osgel esgyrn
Angau a'i chwarelau chwyrn,
Dirfawr fydd hoedl ar derfyn,
Darfod a wna tafod dyn.

Y Drindod rhag cydfod cwyn
A mawr ferw, a Mair Forwyn,
A faddeuo 'nghamdramwy
Amen, ac ni chanaf mwy.

Repentance

Costly office, I sang to her.
I am Morfudd's poet.
By the Man who rules today,
4 *there is a sharp pain in my head for a fair maid,*
and in my brow is a troubling wound:
For a golden girl I am dying.

When Death comes to paralyze the bones
8 *with his whirling bolts,*
life at its end will be a terrible thing.
Man's tongue shall fail.

May the Trinity, to prevent my dwelling in grief
12 *and great turmoil, and the Virgin Mary*
forgive my misguided ways.
Amen, and I shall sing no more.

Drws Gorllewin Mawr, Ystrad Fflur ✧ *The Great West Door, Strata Florida*

Yr Ywen uwchben Bedd Dafydd
Gruffudd Gryg (fl. 1360-1400)

Yr ywen i oreuwas
Ger mur Ystrad-fflur a'i phlas,
Da Duw wrthyd, gwynfyd gwŷdd,
Dy dyfu yn dŷ Dafydd.
Dafydd Llwyd a'th broffwydawdd
Er cyn dy dyfu rhag cawdd;
Dafydd, gwedi dy dyfu,
A'th wnaeth, o'i fabolaeth fu
Dy urddo, yn dŷ irddail,
Tŷ a phob llwyn yn dwyn dail;
Castell cudd meirw rhag eirwynt
Cystal â'r pren gwial gynt;
Dy leau bu deuluaidd,
Dy wrysg, dy gangau, dy wraidd.

  Mae danad ym mudaniaeth
Bedd rwym, nid o'm bodd yr aeth,
Bydaf englynion bydoedd,
Bu ddewr ef, mewn bedd yr oedd,
A synnwyr cerdd a synnud,
A gwae Ddyddgu pan fu fud.
Gwnaeth ei theuluwas lasryw
I'w hael dyfu tra bu byw;
Gwna dithau, geiniau dethol,
Gywirder i Nêr yn ôl.
Addfwyn warchadw ei wyddfa,
Drybedd yw, fodrabaidd dda.

The Yew Tree over Dafydd's Grave

Yew for the best of lads
beside the wall of Ystrad-fflur and its palace,
God's blessing to you, paradise of trees,
4 for growing as Dafydd's house.
Dafydd Llwyd prophesied you
before you grew in the face of tribulation.
Dafydd, after you grew,
8 honoured you – from his youth it was –
as a house of green leaves,
a house with every bough bearing leaves,
a hidden castle for the dead against the snowy wind,
12 as good as the tree of rods of old.
Your parts were noble,
your boughs, your branches, your roots.

There is beneath you in silence
16 the confining grave – not by my will did he go –
of the beehive of englynion throughout the world.
He was brave, he was in a grave,
and you sensed the wisdom of poetry,
20 and woe to Dyddgu when he fell silent.
Her poet's youthful nature made
his generous one flourish while he was alive;
and you, chosen branches, bring
24 faithfulness to the Lord in return.
Gently watch over his grave,
three-footed yew, good maternal one.

  Na ddos gam, na ddysg omedd,
Ywen, odduwch ben y bedd.
Geifre ni'th lwgr nac afrad
Dy dwf yng ngwendre' dy dad.
Ni'th lysg tân, anian annerch,
Ni thyr saer, ni'th ddyfriw serch,
Ni'th bilia crydd, mewn dydd dyn,
Dy dudded yn dy dyddyn;
Ni'th dyr hefyd, rhag bryd braw,
Â bwyell, rhag ei bwyaw,
(Ir dy faich i ar dy fôn)
Taeog na chynuteion.
Dail yw'r to, da le yw'r tau,
Diwartho Duw dy wyrthiau.

Do not move a step – do not learn neglect –
28 *Yew, from above the grave.*
Goats shall not damage or spoil
your growth in your Father's fair land.
Fire shall not burn you, nature's greeting,
32 *no carpenter shall cut, desire shall not break you,*
no cobbler shall strip you, ever,
of your bark in your home.
There will not cut you either – a frightening idea –
36 *with an axe, lest he be beaten,*
– green your burden upon your trunk –
either serf or firewood gatherers.
The roof is leaves, yours is a good place.
40 *May God preserve your miracles from shame.*

Yr ywen fawr, Ystrad Fflur ✧ *The great yew, Strata Florida*

Notes to the Poems

Pererindod Merch ✧ A Girl's Pilgrimage

Dafydd, with his usual hyperbole, declares that his unnamed 'chosen one' has murdered him by rejecting her. As compensation she must make a penitential pilgrimage from Môn (Anglesey) in the north to St David's, Mynyw, in the south, and he exhorts the twelve major rivers on the route to allow her safe passage. To show his good will, he even promises to pay her ferry toll. Finally, Dafydd returns to his legal metaphor with a promise to acquit her and forgive her.

1. **gwawr** 'lady': Literally, 'dawn, sunrise; brightness', but figuratively 'lord, chieftain' or 'princess, lady'.
   cantref: An administrative unit, somewhat analogous to the English *hundred*; literally '100 settlements'.
2. **lleian** 'maiden': Literally 'nun', but at times 'virgin, maiden (like a nun)'.
3. **Non**: The mother of Dewi, St David, named in line 4.
4. **Eigr**: the mother of Arthur, renowned for her beauty.
6. **Mynyw**: an early name (Latin *Menevia*) for the region around the cathedral church of St David's.

'*Y Traeth Mawr, cludfawr air clod*' ✧ '*Y Traeth Mawr – widespread its fame*'

Capel Non a Chroes, Penfro ✧ *St Non's Chapel and Cross, Pembrokeshire*

11. **galanas**: In early Welsh law, both 'murder' and 'compensation paid for murder'.

16. **Menai**: The Menai Strait, known in Welsh as *yr Afon Fenai* 'the river Menai'.

18. **Llyfni**: The Llyfni flows into the sea about eight miles south of Caernarfon.

19, 21. **Y Traeth Mawr, Y Bychan Draeth**: Y Traeth Mawr ('the great strand') lay along the estuary of the Glaslyn where it joined the Dwyryd before the land was reclaimed in the 18th century. Y Traeth Bychan ('the lesser strand') lies along the southern shore of the Dwyryd estuary.

24. **Ertro fawr** 'the great Artro': The two branches of the Artro, formerly *Ertro Fawr* and *Ertro Fechan* 'the lesser Artro', reach the sea south of Harlech.

25. **Abermaw**: Barmouth. The mouth (*aber*) of the Mawddach.

27-28. **Dysynni**: The Dysynni flows into the sea just north of Tywyn in Meirionydd.

29. **Dyfi**: The Dyfi flows into Cardigan Bay at Aberdyfi. It is prone to flooding, especially in its estuary and lower reaches; compare *Y Don ar Afon Dyfi* 'The Wave on the River Dyfi'.

31. **Rheidol**: The Rheidol reaches the sea at Aberystwyth.

33. **Ystwyth**: Prior to the 18th century the Ystwyth entered the sea about a half mile south of the present harbour at Aberystwyth.

35. **Aeron**: The Aeron flows in a southerly arc from Llyn Eiddwen to Aberaeron.

37. **Teifi**: The Teifi forms much of the eastern and southern boundary of Ceredigion, reaching the sea at Aberteifi (Cardigan).

41. **porffor** 'purple': In addition to being a royal colour, purple was the colour of mourning or penitence.

Afon Mawddach, lle mae fferi yn dal i redeg ✧ *The Mawddach, where a ferry still runs*

'Aeron, ferw hyson hoywserch' ✧ *'Aeron, bubbling and loud like a lively lover'*

Llynnoedd Teifi, tarddiad afon Teifi uwch Ystrad Fflur ✧ *The Teifi Pools, source of the Teifi above Strata Florida*

'Teifi deg, tyfiad eigiawn', yn myned i'r môr ✧ *'Fair Teifi, filler of the deep', entering the sea*

Offeren y Llwyn ✧ The Mass of the Grove

In a remarkable extended metaphor, Dafydd describes the singing of the birds in a wooded grove in terms of the service of the Eucharist. In a reversal of the usual format in which the poet sends a messenger to his love, here the speckled thrush, which he describes in some detail as a priest celebrating Mass, attended by a nightingale as acolyte, has been sent by Morfudd to get a pledge of love or faithfulness from him. Tension between the sacred and the profane keeps this poem at a delicate balance and reaches its peak as the priest-thrush elevates the 'chalice of desire and love' in a replication of the most sacred moment of the divine service. While some have interpreted this as verging on sacrilege, it might rather be seen as an example of the subtlety with which Dafydd celebrates the glories of nature and earthly love as a reflection of God's divine love.

6. **arwyddion** 'sacred signs': *Arwydd* 'sign' often has religious overtones.

7. **Pwyll**: *Pwyll* means 'discreet, thoughtful'. If this is a reference to Pwyll Pendefig Dyfed in *The Mabinogi*, it may refer to the fact that Pwyll travelled as far as Annwn, the Otherworld, and back, or it may suggest the character trait of discretion or thoughtfulness implied by his name.

13, 15. **camsai, casul**: The *camsai* 'alb' is a white cassock worn under the *casul* 'chasuble' by a priest at mass.

Y Fun o Eithinfynydd ✧ The Girl from Eithinfynydd

There is some doubt as to the authorship of this poem, but a number of experts argue that it is indeed the work of Dafydd, especially given various independent indications that Morfudd was connected with Meirionydd.

1. **Eithinfynydd**: The name of a farm, medieval enclosures, and hillfort near Tal-y-Bont, Dyffryn Ardudwy, and of another farm between Dolgellau and Llanuwchllyn.

9. **swllt** 'treasure': Literally 'shilling', from Latin *solidus*.

21. **godineb** 'wantonness': In general *godineb* refers to illicit sexual relations outside of marriage. If we understand it here to mean more specifically 'adultery', as it often does, this line could indicate that Morfudd was married when the poem was composed. Lines 16-18, however,

Bryngaer Eithinfynydd ✧ Eithinfynydd hillfort

seem to suggest that Morfudd may be a novice, thinking to join holy orders as a nun, or perhaps she merely has religious scruples when it comes to Dafydd; see also *Cyrchu Lleian* 'Making Advances to a Nun'.

23. **f'anwyl** 'my distress': Dafydd plays on the words *anwyl* 'sickness (physical or mental)' and *annwyl* 'dear, darling'.

Morfudd fel yr Haul ✧ Morfudd Like the Sun

This poem, somewhat longer than most of Dafydd's *cywyddau*, is a superb example of his ability to sustain a metaphor throughout an entire poem. He begins with a series of brief, conventional comparisons to whiteness, and these, with their emphasis on brightness, lead us into the poem's primary image, until at times it becomes hard to distinguish whether he is talking about Morfudd or the sun itself.

Machlud haul o gastell Aberystwyth ✧ *Sunset from Aberystwyth castle*

This is above all a visual poem, with little commentary on his love for Morfudd or on his suffering and almost ubiquitous lover's complaints. Even her resistance or outright rejection of his proffers of love are here manifest only in comparison with the sun as unreachable, literally untouchable. Nor is Morfudd described in any close detail. We are given no color of her hair, her eyes, or her brow, no smile nor shape of her arms or body. She is seen only from a distance, a dazzling radiance as she walks from church to court or as she is envisioned intermittently along the battlements of a castle, like the sun going behind clouds and re-emerging (19-20). Her movements are couched in the vocabulary of sunrise, brightness, and sunset. She does not simply appear in the morning: she *is* the dawn, as Dafydd draws on the ambiguity of the ancient and redolent word *gwawr*, literally, 'dawn' (9), which developed secondary but common senses of 'lord' and 'lady'. Nor does she disappear 'like' the sun as she goes into her house at night: she sets (*ymachludd*) as the sun does, beneath the lintel of the door to her husband's house. Finally, we see her as equal to the sun, indeed as another sun, banishing, for as long as she lives, darkness from the night as the sun does at day.

10. **hyll**: 'ugly, ill-favored; uncouth'. Dafydd contrasts the 'ugly man' she mocks (her husband?) with the poet of lines 11-12, who loves her, i.e., himself.

12. **Gwenhwyfar**: Arthur's wife, Guinevere.

18. **rhwng llan a llys** 'between church and court': Dafydd

Johnston notes that *rhwng* 'between' suggests Morfudd's movement between church and court as mirroring that of the sun across the sky (CDG 708).

34-44. To sustain the Morfudd/sun metaphor, the pronouns *she/her* refer to the sun in this section of the poem, though *it/its* would be more usual in English.

38. **Eluned**: Dafydd may be referring to the fifth-century St Eluned, who, Giraldus Cambrensis tells us, 'refused the hand of an earthly ruler and married instead the King Eternal, thus triumphing in an ecstasy of self-denial' (L. Thorpe, ed., *Journey through Wales*, 92). Does Dafydd see a parallel with his own more worldly situation, in which Morfudd, too, is married to another? **blaned** 'planet': In the Ptolemaic model of the heavens, the sun was thought of as one of the planets circling the earth.

52. **Penrhyn**: *Penrhyn* is a common place name, but this probably refers to the region of Penrhyncoch, around Dafydd's home at Brogynin.

57. **gwawdrydd** 'freely praised': This compound of *gwawd* 'praise; mockery' + *rhydd* 'free, generous, unstinting' might also be interpreted to mean 'freely mocking'. Does it refer to Dafydd's copious praise of Morfudd or to her mockery of him?

Dan y Bargod ✧ Under the Eaves

This poem falls squarely into the class of the humorous *serenade*, a form which arose on the continent in the 13th century, and in which a longing lover complains outside his sweetheart's home. Dafydd's poem shows some general affinities with a passage in the French *Romance of the Rose* (c. 1230), though there is no evidence that our poet knew that work specifically.

1. **Clo** 'lock': Some manuscripts call this poem *Cywydd y Clo* 'The Poem of the Lock.'

4. **aro dy hun** 'wake up!': Literally, 'delay your sleep'.

7. **annwyd**: Ironically ambiguous, *annwyd* can mean either 'emotion, passion, ardour' or 'cold, coldness'.

13. **gwâl**: 'shelter': Literally, 'lair, den'.

27. **y Gaer yn Arfon** 'Caernarfon': The prison in Caernarfon castle is attached to the King's Gate, the castle's main entrance.

42. **ellyll** 'soulless self': Elsewhere Dafydd calls his shadow

Castell Caernarfon ✧ *Caernarfon Castle*

an *ellyll* 'phantom, ghost, spirit', but here he distinguishes his soul (*enaid*), imagined as inside the house with Morfudd, from his physical body out in the cold.

44. **amwyll** 'madness': Literally 'a lack of sense', the negative of *pwyll* 'discreet, thoughtful'. Love as a form of madness was a widespread poetic motif.

Cyrchu Lleian ✧ Making Advances to a Nun

There are several Welsh love poems to nuns expressing unrequited love (see Fulton, *Dafydd ap Gwilym Apocrypha*, 45-55, and 'Medieval Welsh Poems to Nuns', CMCS 21, 87-112). In this poem, Dafydd sends a love-messenger to Llanllugan to fetch a nun for him or, failing that, even the abbess, in lieu, it would seem, of his elusive true love, Morfudd. Morfudd may have been resident at Llanllugan for a time (Dafydd comments elsewhere on her religiosity), or perhaps this poem suggests that it is as futile to send for a nun as it is for him to try to win Morfudd from the clutches of her husband.

The abbey at Llanllugan, founded in the late twelfth century, was one of only two Cistercian nunneries in Wales. Only the church itself remains; a (15th-century?) carved beam possibly from the convent, survives in a private home.

1. **llatai** 'go-between': See the headnote to the following poem.

24. **dyn eglur dâl** 'a clear-browed girl': Comments on a nun's brow became a common humorous trope because her forehead should be covered by her wimple; compare Chaucer's Prioress in the *Canterbury Tales* (General Prologue, 151-55).

29. **câr** 'sister': *Câr* is not gender specific; it denotes both 'kinsman, relative' and 'friend, dear one'.

Trawsbren sgrin y grog allegorïaidd Llanllugan ✧ *The Llanllugan allegorical rood screen beam*

Galw ar Ddwynwen ✧ Appealing to Dwynwen

A motif that developed a particularly Welsh character is that of the *llatai*, the love messenger. Dafydd's creative use of this motif was emulated by numerous later poets. Though occasionally a person, the *llatai* is typically an animal – most often a bird – and occasionally something inanimate. In *Galw ar Ddwynwen* 'Appealing to Dwynwen' Dafydd extends the motif in a remarkable direction, audaciously seeking the aid of the virgin saint Dwynwen as his *llatai* to Morfudd.

St. Dwyn or Dwynwen sought refuge on the island of Llanddwyn, off the southwest coast of Anglesey, where a church and a holy well (now lost) were dedicated to her. She became known, perhaps partly under the influence of this poem, as the patron saint of lovers. As elsewhere, Dafydd walks a fine line using religious imagery and vocabulary to express his all too secular hopes.

6. **Indeg**: Indeg was traditionally one of the three mistresses of Arthur (TYP4 57).
20. **rhod a dyn**: lit. 'between you and a girl'. *Dyn*, lit. 'man' is often impersonal and nonspecific 'one, person, anyone' and can also mean 'woman, maiden, girl', as it often does in love poetry.

Llanddwyn

Adfail Cwm-y-glo Bach ✧ *Ruins of Cwm-y-glo Bach*

23-24. This proverb occurs elsewhere in earlier poetry (EWSP 451, 499; Ford, PLlH 74-5; CBT V 13.22).

25, 46. **mursen** 'prim maid': Derived from Old French *virgene* 'virgin', this term in Welsh developed a range of connotations from 'coquette, flirt' to 'strumpet, whore'. Dafydd uses the same term to describe himself in Merched Llanbadarn 'The Girls of Llanbadarn', l. 29.

32. **Cwm-y-Gro**: Morfudd's home, near Dafydd's home at Brogynin, now called Cwm-glo or Cwm-y-glo; compare *Nant-y-glo* in *Taith i Garu* 'A Journey for Love', l. 40.

gem o Gred 'gem of Christendom': more likely an address to Dwynwen than a description of Cwm-y-gro or Llanddwyn.

54. **Brychan Yrth**: Dwynwen's father, a 5th-century king of Brycheiniog, most of whose ten or eleven sons and twenty-four daughters became saints (TYP4 294-5, WCD 64-7).

55. **creuol gred** 'blood-stained faith': This may be a reference to Christ's blood; however, an 18th-century copy of this poem notes that Dwynwen was martyred beside her well (RWM 2.215), and a 16th-century

poem suggests that blood-stained shirts were left at the well.

56. **ymwared** 'to grant…deliverance': Ymwared 'deliverance, salvation; to deliver, save' may be taken in either a religious or a secular sense.

Cyngor Gruffudd Gryg i Ddafydd ✧ Gruffudd Gryg's Counsel to Dafydd

The englyn attributed to Dafydd appears only in late 16th-century and later manuscripts and may not be original to him, though there is nothing in it that precludes it as Dafydd's own. His poem *Y Gwynt* 'The Wind' seems to refer to a lawsuit against him by Morfudd's husband, Y Bwa Bach (CDG 47.16-17), and *Morfudd yn Hen* 'Morfudd Grown Old' states, *Ni pheidiwn, pe byddwn Bab, / Â Morfudd* 'I would not give up Morfudd if I were Pope' (CDG 150.25-6). The stanza attributed to Gruffudd Gryg occurs only in the earliest manuscript (NLW 1578) containing Dafydd's englyn.

Y Don ar Afon Dyfi ✧ The Wave on the River Dyfi

Large rivers and tidal estuaries were major impediments to travel in the Middle Ages. Crossings could be treacherous at the best of times, and Dafydd exploits this difficulty here and in *Pererindod Merch* 'A Girl's Pilgrimage'. Rachel Bromwich has argued that, in the absence of any other close parallels, the similarity to a poem by Ovid (*Amores* III.6) might indicate the influence of the Roman poet (APDG 72-73). However, it is perhaps equally likely that Dafydd's address to the Dyfi reflects his personal experience, polished by his imagination and wit. Where Ovid curses the river, Dafydd flatters, cajoles, praises, and pleads with the wave to allow him across to see Morfudd. He declares that he is the wave's own poet and that the wave itself is the model to which he would compare all others, including his beloved.

13. **prifwynt** 'cardinal wind': i.e., a wind from one of the four cardinal directions.

24. **Nyf**: Perhaps a reference to the Irish mythological heroine Niamh, the daughter of the sea god Manannán mac Lir, or alternatively, *nyf* 'snow' as a standard of whiteness.

25-26. The foam of a wave was perhaps the most common metaphor to express a woman's fair complexion.

Taith i Garu ✧ Love's Journey

The numerous place names in this poem provide convincing evidence that Dafydd ap Gwilym did indeed live at Brogynin in northern Ceredigion. Many of these places lie within a six mile radius of Brogynin, though he never names it explicitly himself. However, some of these names are open to more than one identification, and our choice depends in large part on our interpretation of the poem itself. The following notes are indebted to R. Geraint Gruffydd's 'Love by Toponymy: Dafydd ap Gwilym and Place-Names' in *Nomina* 19 (1996).

This is a poem with intriguing complexities. Is Dafydd, the perpetually unrequited lover, complaining of that status as he demonstrates his persistent faithfulness by the rigors he is willing to endure? Or is this poem a lament for Morfudd now dead, whom he remembers as he wanders about the hills and valleys in search of solace? Bobi Jones interprets the last four lines as implying a separation of the soul and the body and that Morfudd is dead ('Wrth Angor: Marwnad Morfudd', *Barddas* 173 (1991)). But Dafydd might rather mean his own soul after death in line 51.

7. **Cellïau'r Meirch**: (Map #1) About a mile SE of Brogynin is Ty'nygelli farm, a name recorded the late 16th century; a distant farmstead in Breconshire is called Gellïau'r Meirch.

8. **Eleirch**: (Map #2) An upland township, now Elerch, about two miles NE of Brogynin.

12. **Celli Fleddyn:** (Map #3) This name has not survived, but there is a 13th-century reference to *terra filii Blethin* 'the land of the sons of Bleddyn' in the nearby commot of Genau'r Glyn.

15. **Bysaleg:** (Map #4) The stream now known as Afon Stewi is listed on Saxton's 1578 map as *Massalak*, implying a Welsh form *Masaleg*. (The sounds m- and b- often alternate in Welsh.)

19-20. **Bwlch Meibion Dafydd:** (Map #5) Bwlch Meibion Dafydd is a former name for a stretch of road from Troedrhiwseiri, just above Brogynin, over the hill to the crossroads leading to Elerch.

21. **Y Gamallt:** (Map #6) This is a fairly common place name meaning 'the crooked or curved slope', though there are no known examples closer to Brogynin than about seventeen miles. Gruffydd suggests that Dafydd, in order to satisfy the *cynghanedd*, may have altered the name *Y Geuallt*, which occurs about two and a half miles SE of Brogynin.

22. **Y Rhiw:** (Map #7) *Rhiw* ('[steep] hillside; path or road on a hillside') is a very common place name element, but Gruffydd points out that the name *Penrhiwnewydd* ('the crest of the new road up the hill') within a mile to the SE of Brogynin suggests the possibility of an earlier *Rhiw* or *Henrhiw* ('old road on a hill') nearby.

24. **Gafaelfwlch y Gyfylfaen:** (Map #8) Several pathways intersect at Bwlch y Maen, east of Elerch about two and a half miles NE of Brogynin. In order to make a full line of *cynghanedd groes*, Dafydd cleverly expands the *Bwlch y Maen* ('pass of the stone') by compounding each element with a modifier, giving 'the linking pass of the boundary stone'.

30. **Pont Cwcwll:** (Map #9) The name *Tal Pont Cuculh* occurs in a 14th-century record, and David Jenkins suggests Tal-y-bont about five and a half miles NW of Brogynin (BroDG, 39).

31. **Castell Gwgawn:** (Map #10) *Castell Gugaun* is mentioned in the record cited above, though the name

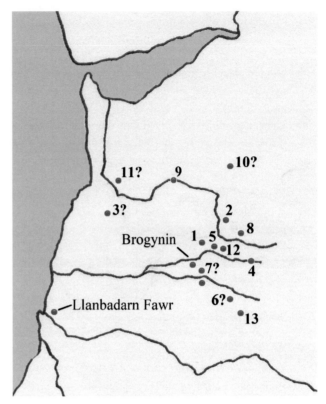

Tirlun 'Taith i Garu' ✧ The Landscape of 'Love's Journey'

has disappeared from the landscape. Jenkins postulates a location in the vicinity of Carreg-y-dwgan / Carreg Cadwgan, about four miles NE of Brogynin (BroDG, 31, 39).

33. **adail Heilin:** (Map #11) Literally, 'Heilin's building'. There is no building in the area by this name, although a 13th-century account refers to *terra Heylin filii Howeli* ('the land of Heilin ap Hywel') in the commot of Genau'r Glyn, and the Gogerddan estate deeds include *Tyddyn Bronheilyn* in the parish of Llanfihangel Genau'r Glyn.

35. **llys Ifor:** No *Llys Ifor* is known in the vicinity of Brogynin, and it is often assumed that there was an

otherwise unknown Ifor who lived in the region. D. J. Bowen suggests that this may be a reference to Ifor ap Llywelyn, Dafydd's patron, and that lines 35-36 have been mistakenly imported here from some other poem by a scribe or reciter who understood *Bysaleg* in line 15 as a reference to Basaleg in Gwent (DGCh, 164).

40. **Nant-y-glo**: (Map #12) Jenkins suggests that this is a name for the valley that runs from Cwm-y-glo past Troedrhiwseiri near Brogynin. Cwm-y-glo (earlier probably Cwm-y-gro) is synonymous with Nant-y-glo (BroDG, 39). There is also a Nant-y-glo in Gwent, some fifteen miles from Basaleg.

42. **heb y llyfr** 'by heart': Literally, 'without a book'.
hoywbwyll Ofydd 'Ovid's lively temperament': Dafydd refers to Ovid no fewer than fourteen times, and here he identifies himself with him.

44. **Gwernytalwrn**: (Map #13) This name is no longer attested in the region, though Penytalwrn is the local name of the George Borrow Hotel about five miles away in Ponterwyd.

50. **fal llwybr Adda** 'like Adam's path': In yet another evocative coupling of the sacred and the profane, Dafydd claims that the physical impression of his lying with Morfudd remains visible on the ground, comparing its permanence with a tradition that nothing grew in the footsteps of Adam and Eve as they left the Garden of Eden.

Dyddgu ✧ Dyddgu

Dyddgu was a significant love in Dafydd's life, second only to Morfudd. Like Morfudd, though for different reasons, Dyddgu, too, proved unattainable. She was the daughter of Ieuan ap Gruffudd ap Llywelyn Llwyd in southwest Ceredigion. Dafydd mentions Dyddgu in nine poems, and from one we learn that she was *o lwyth Tewdwr* 'from the tribe of Tewdwr' (CDG 89.40). The genealogies list Ieuan ap Gruffudd ap Llywelyn as a descendant of Tewdwr Mawr

ap Cadell (DG.net, 'Y Bardd', 17). Another poem suggests that Dyddgu lived in Tywyn, not far from Aberteifi/Cardigan (CDG 46.28).

The present poem begins as an address to Dyddgu's father with echoes of earlier martial praise poetry. Dafydd enumerates the gifts of gold and various drinks he has received from Ieuan, linked together by the repetition of *Dy* 'Your': 'Your gold…/wine…/mead…/bragget'. But suddenly everything changes as the list ends with *Dy ferch* 'Your daughter'! After this, Ieuan is alluded to no more, and Dyddgu becomes the poem's true subject.

The core of this poem is a study in white and black, contrasting Dyddgu's fair complexion and black hair. Lines 33-54 are an extended summary of an episode in the tale of *Peredur*, in which the young hero, after staying one night with a hermit, steps outside in the morning and is transfixed by a raven that had settled on the bloody body of a dead duck in the snow:

> This is what Peredur did – he stood and compared the blackness of the raven and the whiteness of the snow and the redness of the blood to the hair of the woman he loved most, which was as black as jet, and her skin to the whiteness of the snow, and the redness of the blood in the white snow to the two red spots in the cheeks of the woman he loved most. (TA 36-37)

Dafydd simplifies the scene by exchanging the duck for a blackbird and eliminating the raven. A similar state to Peredur's trance is implied by Dafydd in line 50: *Megais hud* 'I am spellbound'.

12. **bragod** 'bragget': a drink made with ale, fermented honey, and spices.

23. **Doethion Rhufain** 'Wise Men of Rome': *Chwedlau Saith Doethion Rhufain* 'Tales of the Seven Sages of Rome' is a 14th-century Welsh version of a collection of tales, originally of eastern origin. Alternatively, the

Ynys Aberteifi ger Tywyn ✧ *Cardigan Island, near Tywyn*

doetheon Ruvein in *Breuddwyd Macsen Wledig* 'The Dream of Maxen Wledig' would also fit the bill (BMW 113; CT 77).

27. **gwialen** 'braid': Literally, 'rod, twig, withe'; see the discussion of *gwialen* in the headnote to *Yr Ywen uwchben Bedd Dafydd* 'The Yew Tree over Dafydd's Grave'.

41. **llwyn Essyllt** 'Essyllt's grove': Dafydd may be alluding to the story of Drystan and Essyllt (Tristan and Isolde), or *llwyn Essyllt* might be a metaphor for 'any treasure or valuable object; here, perhaps, the girl's hair' (Bromwich, DGP 61).

53. **organ** 'organ': The metaphor would seem to be likening her hair, perhaps its braids or ringlets, to the pipes of an organ; though *organ* might be an early example of the sense of 'a part of the body', in this case her head.

Gwahodd Dyddgu ✧ An Invitation to Dyddgu

This poem, too, extols the natural glories of the grove in the woods where two lovers can meet in secret. Dafydd's use of *cymeriad*, beginning successive lines with the same letter or word, provides us with a key to the poem's structure. After addressing it to **Dyddgu**, Dafydd tells us what the invitation is **not** (**Nid**...), and then relates in some detail what sort of a **place** (**Lle**) the 'pleasant grove' is.

4. **dôl Mynafon** 'the vale of Minafon': Dôl Minafon lies along the Rheidol between Llanbadarn Fawr and Plascrug (R.J. Thomas, BBCS vii, 273).

10. **ynyd ciglyd** 'meaty feast': *Ynyd* is Shrove-tide, the three-day period when meat is consumed before the beginning of Lent.

12. **neithior arf barf** 'razor celebration': Literally, 'celebration of a beard weapon', generally interpreted as the celebration of a young man's ritual shave when he comes of age..

30. **neu dri** 'or three': Dylan Foster Evans notes that this is a bit surprising, and he wonders whether Dafydd is referring to the birds or animals there (CDG 685).

Y Gainc ✧ The Tune

No description of Dafydd ap Gwilym's Wales would be complete without music. As evidenced by this poem and elsewhere, the poetry of the *cywyddwyr* was often performed to the accompaniment of a harp, crwth, or other instrument. Here Dafydd conveys his delight in learning a tune on the harp. The poem is replete with musical terminology, some of which is quite technical, e.g., *paradwysgainc* 'tune of paradise', *plethiadau* 'interweavings' *cwlm* 'melody, knot', *sawtring* 'psaltery', *siffancainc* 'tune, symphony', as clarified in Sally Harper's essay, 'Dafydd ap Gwilym: Poet and Musician' (DG.net).

2. **ar dâl mainc** 'at the end of a bench': A passage in a poem by Lewys Môn (*fl.* 1485-1527) suggests that the end of the bench, a place of honour in a Welsh court, was the traditional place in which poems were sung to musical accompaniment.

8. **brwyd** 'loom': Here a synecdoche, *brwyd* is more specifically a term for part of a loom, the heddles which keep the strings of the warp separate so that the weft can be passed between them.

11-12. **semlen** 'a simple thing', **symlyn** 'simpleton': This may refer to the harp tune known as *Symlen ben bys* ('a simple thing for the fingertips'?), first known from 1604. Phyllis Kinney identifies it as a variant of the 16th-century dance 'Mall Sims' (*Welsh Traditional Music*, 62). The title *Symlen ben bys* may have been inspired by Dafydd's poem, or it may simply be a coincidence.

13. **solffeais** 'I sol-fa-ed': Sol-fa was a method for learning to read or sing a tune by assigning a syllable to each note of the scale. Dafydd may have encountered it at Strata Florida Abbey, if not earlier as a child (Harper, p. 42).

25. **Hildr**: Hildr was apparently a legendary harpist; his name appears in a 16th-century list of melodies (Harper, p. 18).

32. **a'i ddeg ewin** 'with his ten nails': Prior to the 17th century the harp was plucked with the fingernails.

34. **cerdd dant** 'music': *Cerdd dant* 'string craft, string music', music played on a stringed instrument, as distinguished from *cerdd dafod* 'tongue craft, poetry'.

Merched Llanbadarn ✧ The Girls of Llanbadarn

In addition to providing evidence that Dafydd ap Gwilym lived in the vicinity of Llanbadarn, this well-known poem presents a delightful version of the comic self-deprecating, frustrated lover. And while it is presumably fictional, it sets out a witty yet entirely believable scenario of a sort that takes place in churches and other such gatherings

Eglwys Llanbadarn Fawr ✧ *Llanbadarn Fawr Church*

everywhere. Dafydd's skilful use of minimal narrative evokes in this seemingly simple vignette the complexity of feelings that arise as young people begin to attract each other.

Lines 29-30 give us the closest thing we have to a contemporary description of Dafydd, though we must keep in mind that it is satirical. A mid-17th-century manuscript (British Library MS Add 14886) includes a note by David Johns, vicar of Llanfair Dyffryn Clwyd:

> *Mi a welais. 1572. hen wraic a welsai un arall a fyssai'n ymddiddan a Dafydd ap Gwilym. hirfain oedd ef a gwallt llaes melyngrych oedd iddo a hwnnw yn llawn cayau a modrwyau arian meddai hi.*

I saw [in] 1572 an old woman who had seen another

who had conversed with Dafydd ap Gwilym. He was tall and thin, and he had long curly yellow hair, and that was full of silver clasps and rings, she said.'

The validity of this note is, alas, highly suspect. That old woman and her informant would have to span the 200 years since the latest likely date of Dafydd's death (c. 1370). Johns' note may reflect a popular tradition regarding Dafydd's appearance, a tradition possibly influenced by Dafydd's description of himself. That self-description, certainly parodic, may reflect contemporary attitudes towards fashion. In 1342 the archbishop of Canterbury complained about the dress of some clerics (DG.net 137.30n; my translation):

'Some men in orders are…making themselves very

conspicuous with hair that they wear nearly to their shoulders in an effeminate manner, and their clothes are more suitable to knights than to clerics, and their curly locks…turn upwards.'

15. **Garwy**: Garwy Hir, a legendary ardent lover, was the father of Indeg, a paragon of beauty and mistress of Arthur.

24. **fy mhlu** 'my feathers': Bleddyn Huws argues convincingly that 'feathers' refers metaphorically to the curls on Dafydd's shoulders, to his beard, and/or more abstractly to his vanity (DG.net 137.24n).

29. **Y mab llwyd** 'the pale lad': Here Dafydd may be hinting at his own name, Dafydd Llwyd fab Gwilym Gam.

35. **rheg** 'gift': *Rheg* developed two opposing senses: 'gift, present' and 'oath, curse, blasphemy; slander, retort'. Both seem apt here.

Cusan ✧ A Kiss

In this poem Dafydd wonderfully conveys the complex feelings of joy and exultation that result from receiving a long-hoped-for kiss. Luned may be her actual name or a pseudonym drawn from the character of Luned, 'a yellow-curly-haired maiden', in the Arthurian tale of *Owain* (TA 74-5). Two formal aspects worth noting are the instances of repetition as noted below and the *cymeriad* linking 25 lines with the initial letter C, echoing the initial sound of *cusan* 'kiss'.

1. **Hawddamawr** 'Hail': *Hawddamor* is a formal word of greeting.

5. **Ffrengig** 'French': Probably figurative in the sense 'excellent, splendid'.

14. **morc** 'mark': A mark was a monetary unit widely used throughout western Europe, valued at roughly 13 shillings and 4 pence.

20. **cwlm cariad** 'love knot, bond': The image is repeated in lines 26 and 35.

23. **canon** 'canon': Here used in the sense of 'rule, law, standard'.

24. **Caerfyrddin** 'Carmarthen castle': A metaphor for the girl's encircling lips; see line 36.

25. **pacs** 'kiss': A direct borrowing from Latin *pax* '(kiss of) peace'. The kiss of peace was a liturgical element of the Eucharist given after the *Pater noster*, the 'Our Father'.

40. **Turel**: Possibly either Hugh Tyrel, a wealthy landowner in mid Wales in the 1330s, or Jean Tyrel de Poix, who in 1359 won an important legal case involving King Edward III (CDG 83.40n).

49. **gwylan** 'seagull': A common image used to express whiteness.

Y Deildy ✧ The House of Leaves

One of Dafydd's favorite motifs is the leafy bower in the woods in which to meet his lover. He mentions a *bedwen* 'birch tree', *cyll* 'hazel', or *llwyn* 'grove' at least once in nearly 25% of his poems. Another favorite image is that of poet as builder or architect. This poem brings the two together with a joyful description of the construction of such a trysting place and the help he will get, with God's support, from the nightingale and the cuckoo, from May and from Summer itself. Yet, as we might expect, his happiness does not last. The tone shifts drastically when Dafydd is stood up, and he vents his spleen at the *deildy* itself.

1. **Heirdd feirdd** 'Lovely poets': While Dafydd may be addressing his contemporaries, it is more likely that he means the birds who sing their *cywyddau* in lines 16-22.

   diledfeirw 'lively': Literally 'not half dead ones'.

23. **Dewin** 'God': *Dewin* 'sage, magician, prophet'. According to an early proverb, *Namyn Duw nyt oes dewin* 'Except for God there is no sage' (e.g., EWGNP V.5c, VIII.4c, IX.61)

30. **Yn gall** 'wisely': *Yn gall* 'wisely, cunningly' completes the thought begun in line 24 (DGP 22).

33. **rhoddi gobrau** 'paying a reward': Literally, 'giving payments'. Poets paid their debts with poems, such as that in the previous 32 lines.

Caru'n Ddiffrwyth ◇ Loving in Vain

Thomas Parry titled this poem *Dewis Un o Bedair* 'Choosing One of Four' (GDG 266), and others have followed suit; however, there is no choice to be made here. Morfudd, Dyddgu, and Elen Nordd have consistently eluded Dafydd, and the odds of winning the fourth are not good. If this poem has an antecedent in the *Gorhoffedd* or boasting poem of Hywel ab Owain (d. 1170), things have gone all topsy-turvy. Hywel boasts with delight about nine women he has loved; Dafydd remains foiled and frustrated (HOG 201).

A motif carried throughout this poem is that of reward or payment. Morfudd and Elen Nordd are both referred to as *anrhaith* 'prize, treasure; dear one; plunder or spoils taken in battle'. Dafydd has always received gold or *ryw beth* 'something' for his poetry (33-34): from Dyddgu he gets nothing but fickleness. According to the conventions of courtly love, a poet who expresses his love to a woman hopes for love in return, even if it is platonic: Elen rewards Dafydd with dry goods. As for the mystery woman from Gwynedd, Dafydd simply insists *Caf... bwyth* 'I shall get a reward', and he clings to his hope (*gobaith*, 51), forlorn as it is.

Dafydd Johnston wonders whether the fourth woman might be the same as the unnamed woman from Gwynedd featured in four other poems, including *Pererindod Merch* 'A Girl's Pilgrimage'. The motif of courtly love in all four suggests a common subject (LU 137; CDG 127-130).

2. **Nantyseri**: Nantyseri has been identified with Cwm Seiri, about half a mile up the river Stewi from Dafydd's home at Brogynin (BroDG, 41, 43).

16. **Robin Nordd**: Robert le Northern was a burgess of Aberystwyth in 1343, perhaps a cloth merchant, as this poem implies.

Trafferth mewn Tafarn ◇ Trouble at an Inn

A perennial favorite, *Trafferth mewn Tafarn* 'Trouble at an Inn' tells of a young man's attempt to spend the night with a beautiful woman he meets at an inn. Dafydd does not give a location for this inn, but we can imagine its like anywhere in Wales that he went. He gives the tale a driving immediacy by presenting himself as the presumptuous and lustful protagonist. From the outset he commands our attention with even such a simple statement as *Cymryd llety cyffredin* 'I took public lodging' by interrupting its three words twice (lines 4-6). The chaotic tumult of the whole poem is heightened by his skilful use of similar *sangiadau* or parentheses that impede the flow of his sentences, making the tension palpable as we witness the seduction scene and step by painful step participate in its disastrous outcome.

We are no longer in the peaceful summer setting of a birch grove, but rather in an urban, bourgeois setting, where food, wine, and pretty women promise to create opportunities for lovemaking. Dafydd gives us a hint of upcoming complications in line 4, *balch o febyd fûm* 'I was a proud youth', but we are led to believe that this time he might be successful when he tells us that any *rhwystr* 'obstacle' to an agreement with the girl has been removed. Not surprisingly, other more concrete obstacles soon make themselves felt. Three proverb-like lines (13, 35, 73) might be read as providing an underlying moral about the foolishness of impetuous young men, and these lead us to the final prayer for God's forgiveness. But let's not let too much analysis diminish our enjoyment of the misadventure itself.

Sarhau ei Was ✧ Insulting his Servant

This poem is another *tour de force* of shifting passions as our poet goes from excessive delight at seeing a beautiful young woman in Rhosyr, to his familiar pining and lovesickness, to hopefulness and flamboyant behaviour as he sends his servant with an extravagant, if presumptuously forward, gift, and turns to vindictive anger when she quite physically rejects his gift.

1. **Gŵyl Bedr** 'St. Peter's Day': 29 June.
2. **Rhosyr**: The Welsh inhabitants of Llan-faes in Anglesey were displaced by the building of Beaumaris castle in 1303 and resettled in Rhosyr (Newborough), with its church dedicated to St Peter.
6. **Enid**: The heroine of the Arthurian tale of *Geraint son of Erbin*, and one of the Three Splendid Maidens of Arthur's Court (TYP4 88).
43-44. **Dafydd…Llwytu ŵr** 'Dafydd…a dark grey man': *Llwytu*, from *llwyd* 'grey' + *du* 'black, dark', puns on his own name, 'Dafydd Llwyd fab Gwilym Gam'.
47. **pum harcholl** 'the five wounds': I.e., the wounds in Christ's hands, feet, and side.
55. **cadas** 'caddice': A worsted cotton thread or soft cloth used for edging.
57. **cwpl** 'couple': An architectural term for one or both parts of a pair of joined rafters.
58. **Madog Hir**: Possibly the poet Madog Benfras. In his false elegy for Madog, Dafydd twice refers to him with the term *cwpl* 'couple' as a metaphor for strength or support (CDG 20.28, 43).

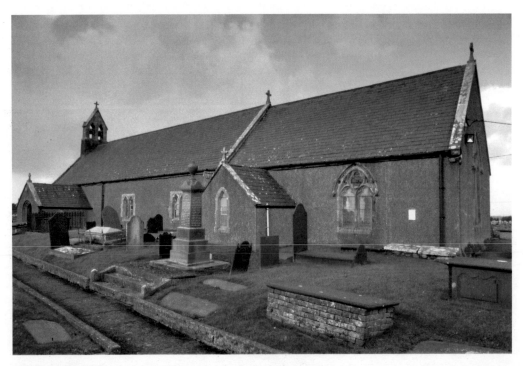

Llanbedr, Niwbwrch ✧ St Peter's Church, Newborough

59. **Einion Dot**: Einion Dot (perhaps from English *tot* 'simpleton, fool') is otherwise unknown.

Gwayw Serch ✧ Love's Spear

The motif of love's wounds is found throughout European literature, and there are some intriguingly close parallels to *Gwayw Serch* 'Love's Spear' in the earlier French *Roman de la Rose*, though there is no evidence of direct influence on Dafydd (DGIA, 230-31). Dafydd's poem complaining about the pangs of love was clearly the inspiration for Gruffudd Gryg's first poem in their poetic debate. Gruffudd begins by taking Dafydd's spear metaphor literally (CDG 23):

> Truan mor glaf yw Dafydd,
> 2 Trwyddew serch trwyddo y sydd.
> * * *
> 12 Eres yw ei fyw efô.

> *It is sad how ill Dafydd is,*
> 2 *there is an auger of love through him.*
> * * *
> 12 *It is a wonder he is alive.*

Dafydd does not name the golden girl of *Gwayw Serch*, but because Gruffudd names Morfudd, some have concluded that she is the subject of Dafydd's poem.

6. **Deinioel Bangor**: The cathedral church at Bangor is dedicated to its founder and first bishop, St Deiniol (d. 584).
8. **Fflur**: A little known legendary beauty; see TYP4 67.
15. **wybr sygnau** 'heavenly signs': i.e., the signs of the Zodiac.
29. **Esyllt**: the Isolde of Arthurian tradition.

Y Cloc ✧ The Clock

Dafydd tells of his dream of a wise girl of noble Welsh lineage, and some understanding of medieval dream theory helps us to understand a number of his points. It was believed that a sleeper's spirit travelled to the person being dreamed about, but only if that person was also asleep would the dreamer be able to see the dreamed. Thus the *angel bach* 'little angel' of line 16 is Dafydd's spirit appearing, in his dream, in the maiden's bed.

But – this is Dafydd ap Gwilym, after all – a church clock shatters his dream. In his subsequent harangue, Dafydd describes a turret clock in considerable detail, although no clock of the sort has been documented in Wales before the 15th century. Indeed the first clocks in Britain date from around 1370. The Salisbury Cathedral clock, restored and still working, is recorded from 1386, and parts of the remains of a similar clock from St David's Cathedral in Wales may date from the 14th or 15th century (CWMW 3, 89, 103). It would seem that Dafydd had indeed at least seen such a clock, perhaps in a monastery, though, of course, that need not have been in Wales. He notes in lines 19-20 that he was far from the girl – perhaps he was in England. But the poem is as likely as not to be fictitious. Might it simply be a clever conceit to honour and amuse the Welsh-speaking folk of Brecon, perhaps one of the ladies in particular.

3. **Rhiw Rheon**: This may be located near where the Nant Rheon springs from the the hillside (*rhiw*) near Aberhonddu/Brecon. The *caer gron* 'round fort' of line 4 may be a reference to the castle of Brecon or perhaps to the circular Iron Age Twyn y Gaer hillfort just above Nant Rheon.
21. **clawdd** 'dyke': Was the dreamer away on the English side of *Clawdd Offa*, Offa's dyke? Alternatively, *clawdd* can also mean 'a wall', and may thus refer to Brecon's oval town wall, a section of which is still called *Clawdd y Gaer*.

Rhiw Rheon(?) a Thwyn y Gaer ✧ *Rhiw Rheon(?) and Twyn y Gaer*

22, 30. **ffriw** 'appearance'; **pryd** 'form': Both *ffriw* and *pryd* can mean 'face', but the early turret clocks had neither hands nor face as we think of them today; rather they rang a bell to mark the hours.

27. **hwyaid** 'ducks': Perhaps a reference to the foliot, a horizontal bar that bobs back and forth on a pivot to control the timing of the clock's escapement.

28. **melinau aflonydd** 'restless mills': The governor had fan blades to control the speed of the striking mechanism.

44. **Eigr**: A traditional beauty and the mother of Arthur, known in English as Igraine.

Y Dylluan ✧ The Owl

Y Dylluan 'The Owl' is one of Dafydd's few poems about birds or other animals that is not about love *per se*, though there is a hint that the owl is preventing him from dreaming of love's enchantment (9). Rachel Bromwich suggests that Dafydd describes the long-eared owl rather than the tawny owl (DGP 98). The owl was associated in classical and medieval thought with both night and death. It was considered a dirty bird which fouled its own nest, and the enmity of other birds was often noted (see lines 33-34). It was frequently depicted with a quite human-like face (31).

21. **Anna**: The mother of the Virgin Mary and the grandmother of Christ.
22. **cŵn y nos** 'hounds of the night': Probably a reference to *cŵn Annwn* 'the hounds of Annwn [the otherworld]' led by Gwyn ap Nudd (40); alternatively, a descriptive term for foxes, which hunt at night.
33-34. In the Fourth Branch of *The Mabinogi*, Gwydion transforms Blodeuedd into an owl: 'And because of the shame you have done to Lleu Llaw Gyffes, you will not dare to show your face in the light of day ever, and that out of fear of all the birds, and there will be enmity between you and all the birds, and it will be their nature to harass you and abuse you wherever they find you' (Mab 106).
40. **Gwyn ap Nudd**: A shadowy mythical huntsman who rides at night with his *cŵn Annwn*.

Y Bardd a'r Brawd Llwyd ✧ The Poet and the Grey Friar

Anti-clericalism and particularly anti-mendicancy were widespread in Europe and Britain in the 14th century. Dafydd composed three poetic conversations with clerics who counsel him to give up wine, women, and song, and look to his soul. *Y Bardd a'r Brawd Llwyd* 'The Poet and the Grey Friar' is by far the longest. In these poems Dafydd participates in the tradition of complaint against the mendicant or begging orders (see M. T. Davies, 'Dafydd ap Gwilym and the Friars', *Studia Celtica* 29 (1995)).

This poem is not a *cywydd*; rather it is Dafydd's only *traethodl*, a simpler forerunner of the *cywydd*. Dafydd may have chosen this form because it was more popular among the ranks of ordinary people than the aristocratic *awdl* and the new *cywydd* with their complex metres. Indeed, it may have been familiar to the friars, even used in their preaching.

Dafydd cleverly parodies the friar's anti-feminism, his negative attitudes towards poets, and his (probably feigned) distaste for sex (Davies 244). He then demolishes the friar's advice with theological arguments, scriptural reference, traditional lore, and simple common sense.

3. **brawd llygliw** 'mouse-coloured friar': i.e., 'grey friar', sardonically identifies the friar as a member of the Greyfriars, the Order of Friars Minor founded in 1209 by Francis of Assisi.
26. **paderau** 'prayers: plural of *pader* 'Pater, Paternoster, the Lord's Prayer; in the plural 'the [prayers of the] rosary; prayer in general'. This word grows in significance throughout the poem.
41-42. While this sounds like a traditional triad, Dafydd might have made it up to give the impression of his 'traditional' learning (CTDG, 176-7).
43-44. **merch** 'maid': The reference is to the Virgin Mary, who was believed to have been assumed bodily into heaven.
46. **tridyn** 'three people': Three biblical figures not born of woman are Adam, Eve, and the high priest Melchizedek (Hebrews 7.3).
58. **segwensiau** 'sequences': a sequence (Latin *sequentia*) is a hymn or chant, sung at mass before the Gospel.
61. **bwyd ac enllyn** 'bread and butter': More literally, 'food and savouries'. Dafydd Jenkins notes of *enllyn*, '[T]his is still a living word for anything eaten with bread, such as butter, cheese, or meat' (*Law*, 341). This would appear to be a reference to Deuteronomy 8.3: 'Man does not live by bread alone' (also Matthew 4.4, Luke 4.4).
63-66. Dafydd echoes Ecclesiastes 3, 'To every thing there is a season, and a time to every purpose under the heaven'.
71. **Ystudfach**: An obscure, perhaps legendary, poet whose name is coupled with those of Myrddin and Taliesin.

Lloer uwch Cors Caron ✧ *Moon over Cors Caron (Tregaron Bog)*

Merch o Is Aeron ✧ A Girl from Is Aeron

The subject of this poem is almost certainly Angharad, the wife of Ieuan Llwyd of Glynaeron and the mother of Rhydderch ab Ieuan, the subject of the following poem. Glynaeron, their home, was near Llangeitho in the Aeron valley. In praising Angharad as the object of his unrequited love, Dafydd is participating in a convention by which the noble wives of patrons were 'courted' by poets according to the tenets of *amour courtois* or courtly love.

4. **Gwawn Geredigion** 'gossamer of Ceredigion': There is a close parallel to this line in Dafydd's elegy for Angharad: *Gwawn Geredigiawn, garw ei dygiad*, 'Gossamer of Ceredigion, cruel was her taking' (CDG 9.66). The elegy may be intentionally echoing this poem from a happier time.

13, 22. **gwayw** 'sharp pain': Literally, 'spear'.

17-20. Compare the reference in *Matthew* 7.26-7 to the foolish man who builds his house on the sand.

25. **oerfel** 'coldness': Literally, 'coldness', but it is also used as a mild imprecation.

Marwnad Rhydderch ab Ieuan Llwyd ✧ Elegy for Rhydderch

Rhydderch ab Ieuan Llwyd (*c.* 1325 – *c.* 1392-1399), an official of Ceredigion and an expert in the law, was descended from the royal line of Ceredigion and, through his paternal grandmother and her mother, from Rhys ap Gruffudd (d. 1197), lord of Deheubarth. Rhydderch lived at Glynaeron, not far from Strata Florida Abbey, and later at nearby Parcrhydderch. The family had long been notable patrons of Welsh poets and were possessors of the invaluable collection of thirteenth- and early fourteenth-century verse known as the Hendregadredd Manuscript. Amongst the later additions to this manuscript are poems to Rhydderch's father, Ieuan Llwyd, and one by Dafydd ap Gwilym to Rhydderch's mother, Angharad Hael, as well as the only known copy of Dafydd's poem to the rood at Carmarthen, possibly written by Dafydd's own hand. It was in all likelihood Rhydderch who commissioned the scribes of Strata Florida to compile the manuscript now known as the White Book of Rhydderch, containing *The Mabinogi* and other tales of Welsh mythological, legendary, and Arthurian interest.

Rhydderch was still alive in 1392 (though he was dead by 1399), long after Dafydd's presumed demise sometime between 1350 and 1370, and the internal evidence of this elegy itself suggests that it is a *marwnad ffug*, a 'false elegy' composed before Rhydderch died. The fourteenth-century *cywydd* poets developed the practice of composing false elegies, and though it can be hard to determine if an elegy is true or false, a *marwnad ffug* generally has a somewhat lighter tone than a true elegy, often with some focus on the theme of love. In this poem we might note that all four times the name Rhydderch appears at the end of a line, it is rhymed with *serch* 'love, affection', reflecting the central theme of the friendship between Rhydderch and his second cousin, Llywelyn Fychan ap Llywelyn Goch ap Llywelyn Gaplan.

2. **och**: *Och* is both an interjection meaning 'Oh!, Alas!, Woe!' and a noun 'a sigh, a moan, a cry of grief or sorrow'.

11 … 13. **Llywelyn … Fychan**: Dafydd and other Welsh poets were fond of the figure of speech known as *trychiad* or tmesis, in which a word or words are inserted between two parts of a name or other compound. Here it is particularly striking that Dafydd embeds Rhydderch's name within the parts of his dear friend's name.

15-16. **Amlyn … Emig**: *Cymdeithas Amlyn ac Amig*, 'The Friendship of Amlyn ac Amig', is an early fourteenth-century version of a widespread tale of extremely close friendship. Emig is a variant form of Amig.

25. **o fedd**: A frisson of ambiguity arises from the fact that the initial mutation of both *medd* 'mead' and *bedd* 'grave' is *fedd*.

41. This line is a response to the question posed in line 9. *Oer* means both 'cold' and, especially in elegies, 'sad, dejected, miserable' (GPC).

Moliant Llywelyn ap Gwilym ✧ Praise of Llywelyn ap Gwilym

Llywelyn ap Gwilym ap Rhys ap Llywelyn ap Ednyfed Fychan was deputy-constable and bailiff of Newcastle Emlyn during the early 1340s, and a direct descendant of Ednyfed Fychan (d. 1246), the powerful *distain* or seneschal of Llywelyn the Great. Dafydd composed two poems to him, this one and an elegy of thirty-five *englynion* lamenting Llywelyn's murder, perhaps the result of a family feud, around 1346. In the latter Dafydd refers to him as *fy ewythr* 'my uncle' and to himself as *nai* 'nephew'. These terms were often used to refer to a more distant relationship than they do today and may only suggest their shared descent from an important family. However, it is possible that Llywelyn was the brother of Ardudful, Dafydd's mother.

Dafydd's *marwnad* for Llywelyn mentions two of Llywelyn's homes by name. Llystyn is located in the parish of Nanhyfer (Nevern) in the cantref of Cemaes, in northwestern Pembrokeshire. To the east, in the cantref of Emlyn is Dôl-goch. A third house was at Cryngae, near Dôl-goch. A 16th-century manuscript copy of this poem appends a note reading 'D. ap Gwilym sang it to Llywelyn ap Gwilym of Cryngae', but the reference to Emlyn in line 4 makes it likely that Dôl-goch is the *llys* being praised (17, 29).

Dafydd may have been fostered with Llywelyn as a youth, but even if not, he undoubtedly spent considerable time with him. In his elegy Dafydd acknowledges Llywelyn as his bardic teacher, calling him *agwrdd udd y gerdd* 'the mighty lord of song' and *prydydd, ieithydd* 'poet, linguist' (CDG 6.7, 6.12). In the present poem, the numerous references to legendary history and traditional narrative reflect knowledge that would be expected of a poet, some of which Dafydd may have learned from Llywelyn.

1. **Llyfr dwned** 'grammar book': *Dwned* is derived from the name of Aelius Donatus, a 4th-century Roman grammarian whose treatise on the basic elements of grammar, *Ars Grammatica*, became a standard school

Abaty Llandudoch, lle claddwyd Llywelyn ap Gwilym ◇ *St Dogmaels Abbey, burial place of Llywelyn ap Gwilym*

text throughout Europe in the Middle Ages. Eventually, any grammar or similar short treatise could be called a *donet* Old French and Middle English and in Welsh a *dwned*. In particular, *llyfr dwned* became the collective term for Welsh treatises on poetry, as compiled in the early 14th century by Einion Offeiriad. Here Dafydd uses the term either as a metonym for his uncle and teacher, Llywelyn ap Gwilym, or alternatively in the sense of an imagined book of the rules of social behavior, according to which guests are drawn to and welcomed at Llywelyn's home.

4. **Emlyn**: Emlyn is the northeastern cantref of Dyfed (Pembrokeshire), bordering Ceredigion along the Teifi.

10. **Lloegr** 'England', **Prydyn** 'Scotland': Dafydd Johnston queries whether this might suggest that Llywelyn fought with Edward III in Scotland in the 1330s (CDG 595).

15. **no chaeth** 'than a serf': I.e., Llywelyn spoke even more gently than a serf, who of course was expected and required to be meek and quiet.

19. **cael … gwisgi ddillad** 'getting … fine clothing': It was

customary to give, or pass down, clothing, especially at celebrations on important holy days.

33. **Gwri Wallt Euryn**: In the First Branch of *The Mabinogi*, 'Gwri Golden Hair' is the name given to the baby found and raised by Teyrnon Twrf Liant of Gwent, who was later renamed Pryderi (38). After Pwyll's death, Pryderi inherits and rules over the seven cantrefs of Dyfed.

35. **Edelffled** 'Aethelfrith': a 7th-century Anglo-Saxon king of Northumbria, remembered as a powerful legendary enemy of the Welsh. An *englyn* by Einion Offeiriad ascribes *Kedernyt Edelfflet* 'the strength of Aethelfrith' to the renowned Sir Rhys ap Gruffudd, who was Llywelyn's brother-in-law (GP 7), and who may be implied here.

37. **Gwyli** 'Gwili': The river Gwili runs through Carmarthenshire and joins joins the Tywi at Abergwili.

40. **Pyll**: Pyll is one of the twenty-four sons of Llywarch Hen whose deaths are lamented by their father in *Canu Llywarch Hen* 'The Poems of Llywarch Hen'.
    Rhodri: Rhodri Mawr ('R. the Great') became king of Gwynedd in 844, king of Powys in 855, and the ruler of Seissyllwg (Ceredigion and Ystrad Tywi) in 872. He was thus the first ruler to hold sway over all three major divisions of Wales.

41. **Beli**: Beli Mawr ('B. the Great'), son of Mynogan, is an ancestor deity from whom many Welsh dynasties traced their lineage.

42. **Llŷr**: Llŷr Llediaith ('Ll. Half-Speech' or 'Half-National'?) was a legendary ancestor, especially of the ruling dynasty of Dumnonia (roughly Cornwall, Devon, and Somerset). In *The Mabinogi* and other sources, he is the father of Bendigeidfran, Branwen, and Manawydan.

Cywydd Mawl i Ifor Hael ✧ In Praise of Ifor Hael

Ifor ap Llywelyn of Gwernyclepa, near Basaleg, west of Newport, was an important patron of Dafydd, who composed six poems to him and a joint elegy to him and his wife, Nest. In these poems, Dafydd presents himself in a role like that of the poets of the earlier Welsh princes, bringing meaningful and very real benefit to his lord through the fame gained through his verse. In this *cywydd* Dafydd bestows upon Ifor the epithet *hael* 'generous' without ever actually using the word in the poem, relying instead on his audience's knowledge of who is meant by 'Rhydderch' (14).

1. **aur** 'splendid': *Aur*, literally, 'gold' or 'golden', is frequently used as a general term of praise.
   maerwriaeth 'stewardship': *Maerwriaeth* is an abstract noun designating the function of the *maer* (8).

2. **diegr** 'not sour': *Diegr* 'sweet, not sour', is translated literally here, as is *dieiddilwr* in line 4, with the negative prefix *di-* in both, using what we might call 'reverse dispraise', a particularly effective form of *litotes* or rhetorical understatement.

8. **maer** 'steward': According to medieval Welsh law, the *maer*, while not one of the traditional twenty-four officers of a king's court, was responsible for the administration of the king's lands (Law 363-4).

12. **bragod** 'bragget': A drink made from a mixture of ale, fermented honey, and spices.

14. **prifenw Rhydderch** 'Rhydderch's epithet': I.e., *hael* 'generous'. Rhydderch Hael ap Tudwal Tudglyd was king of Strathclyde in the late 6th and early 7th centuries. He is named as one of the *Tri Hael Enys Prydein* 'Three Generous Men of the Island of Britain' (TYP4 2).

16. **mab aillt** 'bondman': Literally 'son of a bondman or serf'. With this term and *caeth* 'captive, bondman, serf, slave' (18) Dafydd hyperbolically articulates the traditional relationship of reciprocal dependence between poet and patron.

25. **cyrdd** 'multitudes': *Cyrdd* may be either the plural of *cordd* 'tribe, clan; multitude', with reference to Ifor, or of *cerdd* 'song, poem', referring to the poet himself.

Basaleg ✧ Basaleg, Ifor Hael's Home

Under the guise of sending a greeting to Môn (Anglesey), Dafydd praises Ifor Hael and his court at Basaleg, between Cardiff and Newport. He enumerates the noble pastimes enjoyed there – riding, hunting, hawking, poetry, and games, with particular stress on his friendship with Ifor.

3. **Morgannwg**: Morgannwg, roughly the historic counties of Glamorgan and Gwent, was a kingdom in south Wales formed by the on-again-off-again union of Glywysing and Gwent.

7. **i'm gwlad ni'm gadwyd** 'I am not allowed in my (own) land': This may be a reference to Dafydd's departure (if not flight) from Ceredigion as a result of a legal complaint brought against him by Morfudd's husband, Y Bwa Bach, as alluded to in *Y Gwynt* 'The Wind' (CDG 47).

8. **salm Selyf** 'psalm of Solomon': This reference to the Song of Songs suggests the purity of the love that Dafydd celebrates in this poem.

10. **dyn** 'one': *Dyn* 'man, human being, person, one; woman, girl' is surely intentionally ambiguous here, leading us momentarily to assume a female subject.

22. **claernod saethu** 'shooting at a clear target': This phrase is understood as a parenthetic description of the *clêr* 'poets' who aim their poems at a clear target or subject, in this case Ifor Hael.

29. **Deifr** 'the English': *Deifr* 'Deirans' originally the inhabitants of Deira, a northeastern kingdom conquered by the Anglo-Saxons in the late 6th century. Over time *Deifr* became one of various Welsh poetic terms for the English in general.

41. **ffristial**: 'dice' or a game played with dice, perhaps similar to backgammon.

tawlbwrdd: The word is cognate with Old Norse *taflborð* and may designate a hunt-type board game.

Diolch am Fenig ✧ Thanking Ifor Hael for Gloves

This is the earliest of very few 14th-century poems of thanks for a gift. The genre increased greatly in popularity during the 15th century.

6. **gwëydd gwawd** 'weaver of praise': The reference is to the 'I' of line 5, not to the wife of line 6. Gruffudd Gryg uses the same phrase of Dafydd (CDG 29.23).

7. **Ceri**: a cantref in Powys, cited here both for the rhyme and its distance from Basaleg (about 80 miles).

9-10. **trafaelu** 'to travel', **trafaelodd** 'travelled': Ifor travelled at sea as a merchant and perhaps also as a soldier.

34. **Rheged**: A Brythonic kingdom in the 'Old North' ruled in the 6th century by Urien Rheged.

35. **Taliesin**: Taliesin was a poet of the 6th century who sang in praise of Urien and his son.

38. **'it'**: I.e., the blessing.

47. **Y Wennallt**: The wooded slope named Craig y Wenallt lies about three miles NNW of Basaleg.

57. **calennig** 'gift': Perhaps more specifically a New Year's gift; the word derives from *calan* 'New Year's day, the first day of the year or a month'.

Marwnad Gruffudd Gryg ✧ Lament for Gruffudd Gryg

This elegy for Dafydd's friend and poetic rival was probably composed while Gruffudd Gryg was still alive. Gruffudd also sang a *marwnad* for Dafydd, and half of the manuscripts (written much later) note that Dafydd was alive at the time (GGG, 4). Some have suggested that Dafydd composed this poem as a peace offering to Gruffudd after their *ymryson* or poetic debate, which got quite heated, even if in jest. However, Rachel Bromwich

Eglwys Santes Gathrin, Llan-faes ✧
St Catherine's Church, Llan-faes

argues that since Dafydd's *marwnad*, unlike Gruffudd's, does not so much as allude to that debate, it could just as well have been written before the *ymryson* (APDG, 49). Be that as it may, this poem is, by any standard, a moving tribute to Gruffudd Gryg, in particular as a poet of love.

4. **fal y trywyr marw** 'as for the three dead men': This may be a reference to the widely popular *memento mori* tale

of three men who come across three hideously decomposing corpses and are told that they will end the same (CDG 615).

12. **ysgwir** 'square': Gruffudd was a 'carpenter's square of praise poetry' in that he composed proper poetry according to the rules.

15, 41. **agwyddor** 'alphabet': I.e., a standard, model, or pattern.

20. **Goleuddydd:** In two of the poems in his debate with Dafydd, Gruffudd mentions a Gweirful (CDG 27.50-52, 29.1). Goleuddydd, also the name of Culhwch's mother in the tale of *How Culhwch Got Olwen* (CT 23-24), may be a nickname for Gweirful. Or, like Dafydd, Gruffudd may have sung poems to more than one woman.

38. **Llan-faes**: A Franciscan friary was built on the shore at Llan-faes by Llywelyn the Great in 1237. Nothing remains of it, though its location is still recalled in the names Fryars Bay, Fryars Road, and Fryars Spit. The medieval church at Llan-faes also no longer exists; it was completely rebuilt in the 19th century.

45. **swllt** 'treasured one': Literally 'shilling'.

60. **ofyddiaeth** 'Ovid's art': *Ofyddiaeth*, formed from the name of the Roman poet Ovid (Welsh Ofydd), became a general term for poetry, especially love poetry.

Yr Adfail ✧ The Ruin

Dafydd was fond of poems addressing or conversing imaginatively with others – usually a woman, but otherwise another poet, a friar, a servant, his shadow, various birds, sunshine, and even the abstraction *hiraeth* 'longing'. Here, in dialogue with a ruined house, he recalls the amorous joys he once had experienced there. Responding in a more serious tone, the house touches on the rigors of life in this world, reminding Dafydd of the passing of all things, but without regret.

Adfeilion uwch Llyn Eiddwen, tarddiad yr Aeron ✧ *Ruins above Llyn Eiddwen, source of the Aeron*

Y Drindod ✧ The Trinity

Through a litany of straightforward statements beginning *Da fu* 'Good was…', this instructional poem traces the lineage of salvation from the Trinity through God the Father, to Anna the mother of Mary, to Mary herself, and to Jesus. Drawing on multiple senses of *dwyn* 'to bring, carry, bear, give birth to, endure, suffer', the poem leads us to the hopeful prayer that the Son of Mary will bring us into heaven.

4. **Anna**: St Anne appears in the apocryphal *Gospel of James* (2nd century), but not in the canonical gospels. Dedications to her appear in western Europe from the 12th century.

4. **cyntedd** 'hall': While the modern meaning of *cyntedd* is 'porch, vestibule', in the Middle Ages it designated the upper part of a hall. In *The Mabinogi* Pwyll Pendefig Dyfed receives suitors *y gynted y neuad* 'in the *cyntedd* of the hall' (PKM 13, Mab 28).

23. **gwirswyn gwersyllt** 'truly the spell of a host': The house attributes the storm to malevolent or supernatural forces.

41. **Aeth…â chroes** 'gone to the grave': Literally, 'gone with a cross', an idiom meaning 'laid out for burial' or 'lying in the grave, with a cross on the breast'.

    teulu 'household': *teulu* did not yet mean 'family' in its modern sense, but rather 'household, retinue, warband'. R. Geraint Gruffydd postulates that here it may refer to an otherworldly force, such as the *teulu* of the mythical Gwyn ap Nudd or the *Tylwyth Teg* 'the Fairy Folk' ('Sylwadau ar gywydd 'Yr Adfail' gan Ddafydd ap Gwilym', YB xi [1979], 109–15.).

8, 9. **Duw** 'God', **Duw Iôr** 'Lord God': Here *Duw* means Jesus specifically, thus reminding us of the unity of the Trinity.

10. **pumoes** 'five ages': '(the people of the) five ages', between the Creation and the coming of Christ according to medieval chronology.

Edifeirwch ✧ Repentance

Although a 16th-century manuscript labels this poem as *y kowydd dywaethaf a wnaeth dd ap gwillm* 'the last poem made by Dafydd ap Gwilym', we need not take that statement literally. There is some doubt, also, as to whether it is a true, heartfelt recantation. Rather, it may be another clever way in which Dafydd highlights the suffering that he (or his poetic persona) endures because of his unrequited love for Morfudd.

4. **gwayw** 'sharp pain': Literally, 'spear'; see especially *Gwayw Serch* 'Love's Spear'.

8. **chwarelau** 'bolts': More specifically, a *chwarel* is a bolt or arrow shot from a crossbow.

Yr Ywen uwchben Bedd Dafydd ✧ The Yew Tree over Dafydd's Grave

Central to any consideration of Dafydd's burial place is Gruffudd Gryg's poem addressing a yew tree over Dafydd's grave at Strata Florida abbey, although it is uncertain whether Gruffudd composed it after or before Dafydd died. A large ancient yew near the ruins of the abbey has long been celebrated as the tree under which Dafydd is buried, partly on the basis of this poem. However, there are several reasons to be sceptical. In the 1530s John Leland saw 'xxxix hue trees' there (*Itinerary in Wales*, 1906, 118). A second ancient yew still stands in the churchyard, and in 1854 George Borrow thought that this tree 'appeared to be the oldest of the two. Who knows, said I, but this is the tree that was planted over Ab Gwilym's grave, and to which Gruffydd Gryg wrote an ode?' (*Wild Wales*, 1868, 281). A competing claim, based primarily on a list of the burial places of Welsh poets from around 1600, locates Dafydd's grave at Talyllychau (Talley Abbey) in Carmarthenshire.

Wherever Dafydd may actually be buried, *Yr Ywen uwchben Bedd Dafydd* is considered by many scholars to be a *marwnad ffug*, a false elegy. However, this false status is

Dwy ywen Ystrad Fflur ✧ *The two ancient yews at Strata Florida*

138

Abaty Talyllychau ✧ *Talley Abbey*

based largely on highly subjective criteria of tone and humour, and indeed this poem may not be an elegy at all. The light-hearted tone assumed to stem from implied comparison to the *deildy*, the lovers' 'house of leaves' (39), must be balanced against the likelihood that almost any poem in praise of Dafydd is likely to include reference to his favorite image. This poem is not permeated by the theme of love; rather it is a plea for the yew to protect Dafydd in the grave. In addition, Gruffudd composed a more typical (probably false) *marwnad* for Dafydd. No other poet in the 14th century is known to have written two elegies for the same person.

Perhaps a stronger argument in favor of the authenticity of the poem as postmortem and serious is Gruffudd's comparison of the yew to the *pren gwial gynt* 'the tree of rods of old' in the legend of the three seeds from the Garden of Eden that were planted in Adam's mouth at his burial. This tale had been translated into Welsh as *Ystorya Adaf* 'The History of Adam' by the early 14th century. The seeds grew as three intertwined rods or saplings (*tair gwialen*) that eventually became Moses's staff, which much later was taken to Jerusalem by King David and grew into the tree under which David repents of his sin with Bathsheba and promises to build the temple as penance (GGG 148ff). This tree was incorporated into the temple and eventually became the cross on which Christ was crucified. Barry Lewis suggests that, rather than exalting love's virtues or pleasures, the repeated allusions to the legend draw attention to David's (and hence Dafydd's) adultery. Thus, Lewis sees Gruffudd Gryg as urging the living Dafydd to repent of his amorous ways (GGG 149). But this interpretation ignores the final transformation of the tree into the Holy Cross, which suggests that we might read the poem as a heartfelt expression of Gruffudd's hope that the yew, with a power comparable to that of the Cross to bring about miracles (40), will not only guard Dafydd in the grave, but bring him to faithfulness to God through repentence. This would give an emotional gravitas to a poem that is one of the most moving tributes to Dafydd ap Gwilym.

2. **plas** 'palace': Probably the abbot's house, where notable visitors to the abbey would be welcomed.

5. **Dafydd Llwyd**: As an epithet which developed into a surname, *Llwyd* could mean 'grey, grey-haired' or

Cofeb fodern i Ddafydd, Talyllychau ✧ *The modern memorial to Dafydd at Talley Abbey*

'senior'. The present instance, however, in the sense of 'blessed, holy', refers rather to the biblical King David. Of course, the coincidence of the identical names conflates David and Dafydd in this poem.

7. **Dafydd**: This Dafydd is our poet, well known for his praise of trees.

17. **Bydaf englynion** 'the beehive of *englynion*': This metaphor may refer to the murmuring of Dafydd as he recites *englynion*.

22. **hael** 'generous (one)': i.e., Dyddgu.

26. **trybedd** 'three-footed': Yews grow additional trunks around the original bole. This feature also helps strengthen Gruffudd's equation of the yew and the *pren gwial* 'tree of rods'.

27. **Na ddos gam** 'Do not move a step': This otherwise surprising request is clarified in light of a passage in *Ystorya Adaf*. When David brings the gwial, the rods, to Jerusalem, he lays them in a stone cave, planning to plant them somewhere the next day, but overnight a miracle occurs: 'And then by the divine power of the Cross, ... this is what rose up – the three rods stood themselves and rooted in the stone, and the three intertwined so that they were as one' (YA, Peniarth MS 7.54v).

Afterword: Three Dafydds

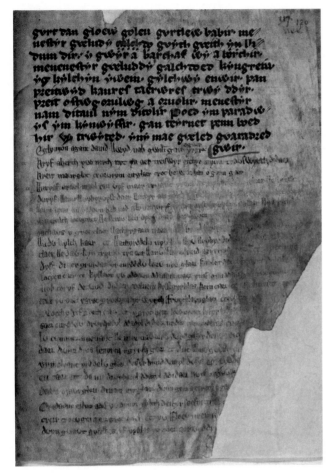

Hendregadredd, fol. 120 ✧ *Hendregadredd, ffol. 120*

Dafydd the Person

Chronologically, we first meet Dafydd ap Gwilym in the pages of the Hendregadredd Manuscript, into which numerous scribes over a number of years in the early fourteenth century copied a precious collection of earlier poetry. On folio 120, someone with a clear but irregular, nonprofessional hand filled the blank lower part of the page and the following two pages with a series of about fifty *englynion*. These are prefaced with the heading *Englynyon a gant dauid llwyd uab gwilim gam yr groc o gaer* 'Englynion which Dafydd Llwyd ap Gwilym Gam sang to the Cross at Carmarthen.' Daniel Huws has suggested that if any of three early copies of poems by Dafydd might be in his own handwriting, this is the most likely candidate (MWM, 221). The ink has faded, the text has suffered considerable damage, and much of it is unreadable; the opening englynion, however, demonstrate Dafydd's confidence as a poet and the linguistic subtlety and fluidity he brings to this sacred topic (CDG 1):

> Cryf aberth yw nerth, nid yn aer—treiswyr
> Eithr mywn trawswyrth didaer,
> Crair mawrglod, croywrym eirglaer,
> Crog bedwarban o gan Gaer.

> Lluniaf arawl mawl can wyf maer—ar wawd
> I'r wiwdeg fygrddelw glaer,
> Lle breisgdwrf llanw llwybr wysgdaer,
> Llathr amgylch cyfrestrfylch Caer.

> *Strong sacrifice is the strength, not in the oppressors' battle,*
> *but in a powerful and gentle miracle,*
> *of a relic of great fame, pure, strong and much praised,*
> *the four-pointed cross of resplendent Caer.*

I will make a claim of praise, since I am steward of song,
for the fitting, fair, beautiful, clear image,
where the tide's fierce course makes a great noise,
gleaming around the row of battlements at Caer.

In the mid-fourteenth century this manuscript was in the possession of Ieuan Llwyd of Glynaeron, whose family, descendants of the Lord Rhys of Deheubarth, had been important patrons of poets for generations. The manuscript also contains a copy (in a different hand) of Dafydd's elegy (CDG 9) for Angharad, Ieuan's wife, to whom he also may have sung *Merch o Is Aeron* 'A Girl from Is Aeron'. In other manuscripts we find Dafydd's false elegy for Angharad's son, *Marwnad Rhydderch ab Ieuan Llwyd* 'Elegy for Rhydderch', who commissioned the famous Llyfr Gwyn Rhydderch, the White Book of Rhydderch. On a blank page in this latter manuscript someone added the only known copy of four *englynion* celebrating a kiss (CDG 84), which are attributed to Dafydd and which share some of the images in *Cusan* 'A Kiss'. It is possible that Dafydd himself was familiar with this manuscript; he frequently cites names and images from *The Mabinogi* and the other tales it contains.

Ieuan Llwyd had deep family ties to Strata Florida Abbey, founded and endowed by the Lord Rhys, about ten miles from Glynaeron. While there is no contemporary documentary evidence, it is not unlikely that Dafydd received at the abbey some schooling in Latin and perhaps writing. Had he learned to write there, it would have been in a hand similar to that of the poem to the Carmarthen cross (MWM, 221). And indeed the evidence seems to point in the direction that Dafydd is in fact buried at Strata Florida.

Unfortunately, we know neither when Dafydd was born nor when he died, though on the basis of the relatively few datable references and identifiable personal names as occur in his poetry we can approximate the 1340s as the period of his greatest activity. His birth, then, must have been no later than 1325, which would make him an extraordinary young prodigy – a possibility we can not entirely rule out but should not assume. Sometime around 1310-1320 might be more reasonable. Estimates of his death range from *c.* 1350 to *c.* 1370. His father was Gwilym Gam ap Gwilym and his mother was Ardudful, perhaps the daughter of Gwilym ap Rhys. The lineage of both of Dafydd's parents can be traced back to Ednyfed Fychan, seneschal to Llywelyn the Great, many of whose descendants, like Sir Rhys ap Gruffudd and Llywelyn ap Gwilym, Dafydd's uncle, became important regional and local figures in the fourteenth century.

Most of what we know about Dafydd's life must be gleaned from his poetry, which by its very nature can be unreliable in factual matters, especially in regard to his love life. But we do get more than a general, if fragmentary, picture of his life. His poetry is sufficiently wide ranging that we also get to know his interests, his understanding of the emotional complexities of life, and his love of the natural world around him, especially birds, of whom he was an astute observer. In more concrete terms, we can locate important parts of his life through his references to places and people. He reveals a detailed knowledge of the geography of northern Ceredigion. Most particularly, the landscape around Penrhyncoch that he traverses in *Taith i Garu* 'Love's Journey' allows us to say with some confidence that Brogynin was indeed his home, as tradition has held since the fifteenth century. Brogynin was formerly in the parish of Llanbadarn Fawr, about five miles from the church, and we can thus take Dafydd at his word that he spent his Sundays there, though he may be exaggerating his attention to girls and inattention to God in *Merched Llanbadarn* 'The Girls of Llanbadarn'.

Dafydd's attachment to the Llanbadarn-Aberystwyth area is further demonstrated by the names of two husbands which appear in official records. Y Bwa Bach, as he names Morfudd's husband in two poems (CDG 47, 110), is undoubtedly the *Ebowa Byghan* (Y Bwa Bychan) who in

1344 appears as surety for a fine to be paid by one Howel ap Gronow for stealing two silver cups. As it happens, those cups were stolen from Robert le Northern, a burgess and bailiff of Aberystwyth who swore fealty to the Black Prince in 1343. He is clearly Robin Nordd, Elen's husband in *Caru'n Ddiffrwyth* 'Loving in Vain'. Dafydd also composed an *awdl* (CDG 7) in praise of another of the guarantors of Howel ap Gronow's fine, Ieuan Llwyd ab Ieuan Fwyaf, who served as beadle, reeve, and constable in nearby Llanfihangel Genau'r Glyn in the 1330s and 1350s. Dafydd concludes this poem by naming Ieuan as his foster father. Two other prominent male figures played significant roles in shaping Dafydd's life. The brother of Dafydd's mother, Llywelyn ap Gwilym ap Rhys of Dôl Goch in Emlyn was constable of Newcastle Emlyn in 1343. As a boy Dafydd may have been fostered with his uncle, a common practice at the time, and it may even have been Llywelyn who lit the fire of poetry under his young nephew: *Ys difai y'm dysgud* 'Faultlessly you taught me', Dafydd says in his elegy composed after Llywelyn was murdered in 1346, and he calls him *Cerddwriaeth ddoethineb* 'the wisdom of the art of poetry (CDG 6.22, 102). In *Moliant Llywelyn ap Gwilym* 'Praise of Llywelyn ap Gwilym', Dafydd designates him *Llyfr dwned Dyfed* 'Dyfed's grammar book', that is, the expert to consult about the art of poetry.

Another patron of Dafydd was Ifor ap Llywelyn ab Ifor ap Llywelyn of Gwernyclepa, near Basaleg in Morgannwg. Little is known about Ifor, but Dafydd composed seven poems to him. In *Cywydd Mawl i Ifor Hael* 'In Praise of Ifor Hael', Dafydd cleverly bestows on him the epithet *Hael* 'generous', without so much as uttering the word itself. We do not know how much time Dafydd spent with with Ifor and his wife Nest, but Dafydd's praise of Ifor's home, Basaleg, and his repeated reluctance to leave Ifor strike one as both fulsome and heartfelt.

This brings us to the somewhat more elusive figures who made Dafydd immortal. Beyond doubt, the most important people in Dafydd's creative life were the women he sings about with his inimitable potpourri of love, delight, hope, despair, frustration, and then more hope. It was formerly believed that Morfudd and Dyddgu were imagined stereotypes created by Dafydd to present a contrasting pair: Morfudd, *fy rhiain aur* 'my golden girl', and Dyddgu, *â'r gwallt lliwddu lleddf* 'with the smooth, black hair'. However, careful research has turned up evidence that these were both real women, not just fictional types standing in for someone Dafydd might have known or would have liked to know. This is not to say that everything Dafydd says about them, or about his relationships to them, is literally true, but it adds multiple layers of complexity to the poems.

Judging by the frequency with which she appears and the range of emotions she evokes in him, Morfudd was Dafydd's greatest love, though she proved perennially elusive. Her name occurs in thirty-six out of 151 poems, and her husband is named twice and alluded to as *yr Eiddig* 'the Jealous One' more than a dozen times. And, of course, other poems may be about her although they do not name her. We have already met her husband in the region around Aberystwyth; *Taith i Garu* 'Love's Journey' places Morfudd, too, in Dafydd's neighborhood, where he would wander

> I geisio heb addo budd
> Gyfarfod â gwiw Forfudd.

> *to try, without promise of success,*
> *to meet with lovely Morfudd.*

In *Y Cariad a Wrthodwyd* 'The Rejected Lover' (CDG 118), Dafydd names her *Morfudd ferch Madawg Lawgam* 'Morfudd daughter of Madog Lawgam', though Madog Lawgam is otherwise unknown. Whether Morfudd originally came from Eithinfynydd is also uncertain, for there is some doubt as to whether Dafydd is the author of *Y Fun o Eithinfynydd* 'The Girl from Eithinfynydd', in which

Cors Caron yn y gaeaf ✧ *Cors Caron in winter*

her name occurs. Such narrative as we can piece together about her comes, therefore, from the poetry itself, which suggests that he loved her before she was married, that he was heartbroken when she did marry, and that he may have had some, shall we say, occasional amorous success with her after she was wed, but that their relationship throughout was very much on-again, off-again – mostly off. And we should keep in mind that Dafydd may be creating much of that narrative for purely poetic purposes.

Dyddgu, whom Dafydd names along with Morfudd and Elen in *Caru'n Ddiffrwyth* 'Loving in Vain', and to or about whom he sings nine other poems, lived with her father in Tywyn, on the outskirts of Aberteifi (Cardigan). In *Dyddgu*, Dafydd begins by addressing her father, Ieuan ap Gruffudd ap Llywelyn, a descendant of the important and ancient lineage of Tewdwr Mawr. Surely to gain Ieuan's favour the poem is initially couched much in the style of the praise poetry of previous centuries, though it soon shifts to Dafydd's true interest – Dyddgu herself. Her social status was somewhat higher than that of Dafydd, and thus he couches his poems to her in a different tone than those to Morfudd. In most of his poems to Dyddgu there is a touch or more of attention given to her lineage and nobility, or else the imagery he uses is pertinent to the interests or pastimes of the aristocratic class. It may be no accident that the *llatai* 'love messenger' that Dafydd sends to her is a roebuck, the prize animal of the noble hunt (CDG 46). Dafydd may even be gently addressing their relative status in *Y Gainc* 'The Tune', when he offers a simple harp melody (*symlen*) in praise of an *edlingferch* 'noble girl' who turns out to be Dyddgu.

Dafydd the Poet

Dafydd ap Gwilym's grandparents were perhaps old enough to remember the days of Llywelyn ap Gruffudd, when it seemed possible, perhaps even likely at times, that Wales could remain largely independent and be ruled by Welsh princes. If they were too young to have lasting memories of such promise, they certainly knew the dark years after 1282 when the heavy burden of English authority was made visible in the ring of massive castles Edward I built to be dauntingly domineering over both the landscape and the minds of the Welsh people. Dafydd's parents, and Dafydd, too, grew up in a Wales in which many of the ancient structures of Welsh society had been destroyed outright or had weakened and crumbled for lack of a solid foundation. The Welsh princes and their families had been killed in battle, executed, or, in the case of their wives and daughters, confined and cloistered in nunneries far from Wales.

But life must go on, and while the upper levels of government were exclusively English, there grew a need for administrators and mid-level officials at regional and local levels to regulate, and of course to communicate with, the Welsh populace. This need was filled in part by the Welsh landed gentry, some of whom were more distant surviving relatives of the royal families and their top officers, especially the influential descendents of Ednyfed Fychan. As well as administering the king's government, these *uchelwyr* 'high(-born) men' served as buffers, shielding as best they could the Welsh from the worst or most immediate effects of oppression.

Simultaneously, the *uchelwyr* took pride in and nurtured the memory of the Welsh past, the dignity of their lineage, and the continuity of their own deep traditions. Pride of place among those traditions went to the art of poetry. Where the highest ranks of professional poets had formerly sung to and been supported by a particular prince or lord, the loss of that support now required them to travel from court to court, singing the praise and lauding the descent of the *uchelwyr*. In turn, many of the *uchelwyr* took pride in their own knowledge of the complexities of Welsh verse.

Dafydd ap Gwilym grew up and travelled extensively in this world, sharing his poetry at various courts. He often alludes to the rewards he is given for his poems, as in *Dyddgu* and *Diolch am Fenig* 'Thanks for Gloves', but because of his ambiguous status as both a poet and a member of a noble family and because the largest part of his poetry is about his love life rather than his patrons' praise, one hesitates to call Dafydd a professional poet. His paternal line records two, possibly three, poets, including Cuhelyn Fardd, whom R. Geraint Gruffydd suggests might have been the *pencerdd* 'chief poet' of Rhys ap Tewdwr, king of Deheubarth in the eleventh century (APDG 13). However, there is no indication that Dafydd descended from a line of hereditary poets who passed down their craft from generation to generation, like Meilyr Brydydd, his son Gwalchmai, and three sons of Gwalchmai – Einion, Meilyr, and possibly Elidir Sais – in the twelfth century. With Dafydd we are on firmer ground if we accept his own word that some of his learning at least came from his uncle, Llywelyn ap Gwilym.

Wherever and whenever Dafydd received his early education, there can be no doubt that he was fascinated and undoubtedly at times obsessed by language. Virtually all of his poetry shows an inventive mind drawing on many sources for material and playing with both the poetic vocabulary inherited from the past and the language spoken around him, including a willingness to borrow from English and French either simply for effect or to fulfil the metrical requirements of a line. His mastery of both *awdl* and *englyn* shows that he was well trained in the methods and poetic traditions of an earlier age. Acquiring that skill and knowledge alone would take years of careful, intense study.

But there was a new movement afoot in the mid fourteenth century, one that allowed Dafydd's linguistic acuity and his creative imagination a freer rein than was accessible to poets of the past. Dafydd and a number of other young poets of the mid century adopted the *cywydd deuair hirion*, generally called simply the *cywydd*, as their metre of choice. But the greatest innovation in the poetry of the *cywyddwyr*, the 'cywydd poets', was in the matter of subject and theme, and here Dafydd's influence was profound. There had been some earlier poets who sang of love, either as a platonic tribute to a noble lady or, occasionally, in what we today might call a love poem. The best known example of the latter is the poet-prince Hywel ab Owain Gwynedd, who composed five poems to unnamed women and in his *Gorhoffedd* or boasting poem celebrates eight women by name (HOG 201). It may have been Hywel's status as prince rather than professional poet that allowed him the freedom to step outside the usual range of themes, though, to be sure, we do not know the nature of the poetry that might have circulated without being copied into manuscripts.

In the mid fourteenth century, Dafydd became the love poet *par excellence* and the central figure in debates about the acceptable topics for poetry. The *ymryson* or poetic debate between Dafydd and Gruffudd Gryg, consisting of four poems each, begins with Gruffudd's reaction to Dafydd's *Gwayw Serch* 'Love's Spear'. Gruffudd sneers, certainly in jest, at Dafydd's complaints about the 'spear pangs' of love, calling them *mawr o gelwydd* 'a great lie' and Dafydd *prydydd brad* 'a poet of deceit' (CDG 23.35). Dafydd replies (CDG 24.5-6):

Nid mwy urddas, heb ras rydd,
Gwawd no geuwawd o gywydd.

There is no more nobility, apart from abundant grace,
in a poem of praise than in a fictitious cywydd of love.

The argument is never resolved; it devolves into an increasingly sharp, satirical flyting rather than a serious debate about the proper subjects for poetry, each poet ultimately claiming, as the greatest possible insult, to be the other's father.

The practice of singing *marwnadau ffug* 'false elegies' to each other may have been a way for the early *cywyddwyr* to hone their craft, to develop, somewhat playfully and perhaps in competition with each other, a style in the new metre that would be suitable for more serious elegies when needed, or perhaps they simply provided a way to offer compliments to a friend or patron. We know that some elegies are premature, for Dafydd wrote elegies for Gruffudd Gryg and Madog Benfras, and Gruffudd and Madog each wrote an elegy for Dafydd. Someone was still alive, we just don't know for sure who. A powerful side effect of these false laments is that they throw into doubt the ante- or postmortem status of other elegies. It is now generally accepted that Dafydd's elegy for a third poet, Gruffudd ab Adda (CDG 21), is also false, as well as his *Marwnad Rhydderch ab Ieuan Llwyd*.

Of the three contemporary poets who wrote elegies for Dafydd, Iolo Goch's, with its less personal tone, is the most likely to be a true lament (LU 149). But whether they were composed before or after his death, there is one motif common to all three that highlights Dafydd's prominence among the early *cywyddwyr*:

Disgybl wyf, ef a'm dysgawdd,
Dysgawdr cywydd ... .

I am his disciple, he taught me,
a teacher of the cywydd ... .
       – Gruffudd Gryg (GGG 4; GDG 427)

Da athro beirdd, dieithrach
No dyn a fu, a Duw'n fach.

A good teacher of poets, more exceptional
than anyone who ever lived, and God is dear.
       – Madog Benfras (GMB 4; GDG 425)

Athro grym glewlym gloywlef
A thëyrn oedd, aeth i'r nef.

A strong, brave, keen, clear-voiced teacher
and lord he was. He went to heaven.
       – Iolo Goch (IGP 90-91; GDG 423)

Dafydd was an especially innovative master of extended metaphor. In addition to *Morfudd fel yr Haul* 'Morfudd like the Sun', a descriptive *tour de force* exploring a single metaphor throughout the poem, *Offeren y Llwyn* 'The Mass of the Grove' presents us with a metaphor that offers insight into his love of the natural world and into the very heart of his exaltation of earthly love and human desire. The *llwyn*, of course, is the wooded grove where he met, or hoped to meet, any of various girls, though he clearly delights in the setting for its own sake, as well. The remarkable fact about the poem, however, is that he builds a detailed metaphor that describes that worldly – one might easily say, profane – location as a sacred place at the most sacred of moments. God's creation, Dafydd strongly implies, is equally sacred and should be understood as such. The speckled thrush, presented as a priest, raises aloft the *caregl nwyf a chariad* 'the chalice of desire and love', as the nightingale rings the sanctus bell. Skirting the edge of sacrilege, Dafydd accomplishes a poet's ultimate task – making us see and understand the world, and perhaps ourselves, from a new perspective.

Moryd Dyfi ✧ *The Dyfi estuary*

'Dafydd' the Persona

Most of Dafydd's poems, especially the love poems, are presented from a first-person perspective. One difficulty we may have as readers is distinguishing between Dafydd ap Gwilym and 'Dafydd' the persona, the 'I' who appears in the poems. Many of those named in his verse are identifiable as real people, rather than as poetic fictions. It is tempting, then, to assume that the events in the poems are true and reveal Dafydd's biography. But the 'Dafydd' in a poem is not the same as Dafydd himself. (I shall use inverted commas to distinguish the poetic persona 'Dafydd' from the actual poet.)

Any poem is fictional to a degree. Poems of praise, for example, may express a poet's true feelings of respect, honour, and love of a patron, but through hyperbole and exaggeration. The same is even more true of Dafydd's love poetry. We do not get to know the actual Morfudd, though she may indeed have lived at Cwm-y-glo and had (one would hardly dare to doubt) golden hair. Rather, the 'Morfudd' we meet in the poems is the idealized but problematic lover that 'Dafydd' certainly, and Dafydd in all likelihood, loved and pined after. 'Dafydd' is the medium through which Dafydd expresses himself to us.

Dafydd's persistent theme is love, its joys, glory, sharp pains, and heartache. The emotions and the effects of love that he portrays may, indeed, have been very real in his life, while the events described may be wholly or partly fictional. He exaggerates both an event and his emotional response to it in order to construct an engaging poem. Without taking it all too seriously, for Dafydd himself keeps humour close to the surface, we gain an understanding of the complexities of love and longing through the cumulative effect of multiple poems, as each poem reflects a different facet of the gem he cuts so brilliantly.

Enlisting himself as 'Dafydd', Dafydd skilfully conveys the often comic sufferings of the lover. Such suffering, of course, is not amusing to any of us when we encounter it in our own love lives, but Dafydd, becoming his own foil, helps us to recognize in ourselves an emotional complexity ranging from carnal desire to unalloyed joy, from resigned adoration from afar to frustration and anger. Even the religious ecstasy in *Offeren y Llwyn* 'The Mass of the Grove' is occasioned, in the poet's imagination, by the fact that Morfudd sent the thrush to him as her *llatai*, and this accounts for much of the poem's exultant tone. *Y Deildy* 'The House of Leaves' begins in similar delight as he invites his *cariad*, his darling, *i dŷ dail a wnaeth Duw Dad* 'to a house of leaves God the Father made.' But suddenly, in its last lines, 'Dafydd' erupts in a flash of anger when Morfudd or Dyddgu, or whoever he had hoped to meet, presumably fails to show up, and he repudiates both *llwyn* and *deildy*. A sudden, unexpected shift such as this reveals the careful control that Dafydd maintains over the tone and effect of his poetry through his main character, 'Dafydd'.

The question of the relationship between Dafydd and his persona also arises in a poem such as *Dyddgu*. Dafydd begins this poem addressing and praising Dyddgu's father, Ieuan ap Gruffudd ap Llywelyn Llwyd, and he enumerates the payments he has received from Ieuan for his poetry, ending that list with Dyddgu herself. However, it is absurd to think that Dafydd could seriously claim Ieuan ap Gruffudd's daughter as a reward or payment for any number of poems. Perhaps we might understand it as a courtly love poem, in which the poet has no expectation of anything more than friendship from the woman he praises. On the other hand, the fiction of courtly love in this instance is complicated by the fact that he is expressing love for his patron's daughter, presumably unmarried, not his wife, as he does for Angharad, Ieuan Llwyd's wife, in *Merch o Is Aeron* 'A Girl from Is Aeron'. And as his seven other poems to Dyddgu testify, it seems clear that Dafydd was not interested in her solely as a subject for merely platonic praise. Is this poem possibly an oblique approach to sound out how Ieuan might respond to Dafydd's love for or attraction to his daughter? Might he have had hopes above his own social status, as is implied in *Caru Merch Fonheddig* 'Wooing a Noble Girl' (CDG 87.9-10), which might very well be a response to *Dyddgu*:

Rhy uchel, medd rhai, uchod
Y dringais pan gludais glod.

Too high above, some say,
I climbed when I sang your praise.

Could *Dyddgu* have been recognized by Ieuan, by Dyddgu herself, and by Dafydd's wider audience purely as a courtly poetic conceit, cleverly structured simultaneously to flatter Ieuan with echoes of the heroic poetry of a previous age, and to praise his daughter's beauty with a comparison drawn from a chivalric Arthurian tale from that same age? To put it another way, who is the sleep-deprived, lovesick 'I' of this poem, 'Dafydd' or Dafydd? Again, a hint may come at the end of the poem, when he throws the question open to the critics, i.e., his audience:

Barned rhawd o'r beirniaid draw
Ai hywaith, fy nihewyd,
Ymy fy myw am fy myd.

Let yonder crowd of critics decide:
Is it worth it – she is my ardent desire –
for me, my living in longing for my love?

This final question draws attention to Dafydd's reputation as the poet of love in his role as 'Dafydd', the perennial suffering lover. The courtly love poet, in Welsh no less than in French, is caught in a cleft stick. He must express his absolute and unwavering love for a woman whom everyone knows is unattainable to him because of her rank, because she is married, or both. Dafydd, however, takes that convention and asks, How do we, or at least, how can I resolve this problem in the real world? One is reluctant to deny that Dafydd may indeed have had an amatory love for Dyddgu, as he did for Morfudd, and thus the distinction between poet and persona becomes a central problematic conundrum in this poem.

In many poems Dafydd skilfully negotiates a delicate balance between the voice of the persona and the voice of the poet. He often uses *sangiadau* to give one an opportunity to comment on the other, though it is not always clear which is which. A passage from *Galw ar Ddwynwen* 'Appealing to St Dwynwen' illustrates this interplay of narrative voicing:

Y fron hon o hoed gordderch
Y sydd yn unchwydd o serch,
Hirwayw o sail gofeiliaint,
Herwydd y gwn, hwn yw haint,
Oni chaf, o byddaf byw,
Forfudd, llyna oferfyw.

From longing for a lover this breast
is nigh bursting with love
– long-lasting pain based in anxiety –
because I know – this is a sickness –
that if I do not get – if I live –
Morfudd, then life is in vain.

The statement by 'Dafydd' is straightforward, if a bit excessive (as lovers are wont to be). While we might assume the interpolated *sangiadau* are 'Dafydd' revealing his inner thoughts, we might also read them as Dafydd, in a secondary voice, interjecting his own commentary, ambiguously defining love longing as 'long-lasting pain based in anxiety' and a *haint* 'a fatal disease, sickness', finally suggesting sardonically with *o byddaf byw* 'if I live' that such love sickness is not literally life threatening. The effect of these parentheses is to help us to step back a bit from the persona's running narrative to get momentarily a more distant, though not necessarily more objective, perspective from the poet.

Dafydd extends the range of his persona in a new mode of *cywydd*, making himself, as 'Dafydd', the ineffectual protagonist of short narrative *fabliau*-like poems. The *fabliau* was a genre of comic, often risqué tale in verse popular in France in the twelfth and thirteenth centuries, and that spread to Britain in the fourteenth. A primary theme was a satirical view of marriage and adultery in a bourgeois rather than an aristocratic milieu. In *Trafferth mewn Tafarn* 'Trouble at an Inn' and *Sarhau ei Was* 'Insulting his Servant', both narrator and persona are even more comic than in the love poems. Here Dafydd deploys *sangiadau* liberally, but with subtlety and precision. We find ourselves at an inn, rather than a noble court, observing the exploits of an over-confident, proud young man intent on spending lavishly to impress a girl and with luck get into her bed. In this setting, Dafydd repeatedly offers wry but telling commentary on the foolishness of 'Dafydd', as in *Trafferth mewn Tafarn*:

Cymryd, balch o febyd fûm,
Llety, urddedig ddigawn,
Cyffredin, a gwin a gawn.
* * *
Hustyng, bûm ŵr hy astud,
Dioer yw hyn, deuair o hud.

I took – I was a proud youth –
public – dignified enough –
lodging, and I got some wine.
* * *
I whispered – I was a bold, eager fellow,
that's for sure – two words to charm her.

In many poems it is more difficult to tease apart the voices of Dafydd and 'Dafydd'. It often comes down to a matter of tonal shifts that clarify for us the lessons to take away from the levity. Ultimately Dafydd's presentation of himself as a figure of fun brings us beyond laughter to the recognition in ourselves of the complex emotions that so often accompany the experience of love, whether that love is accepted or rejected.

A Brief Introduction to Welsh Metrics

Early Welsh poetry, from the ninth century, perhaps as early as the the sixth, shows a sophistication, complexity, and polish that is remarkable, given that the language itself was just evolving from the Brythonic language that had been spoken earlier in Britain. Over time the principles and rules governing poetic structure became increasingly elaborate, as poetry itself played a role central to the very structure of society. Poets composed songs of praise that articulated the historical and genealogical bonds that held rulers responsible for the well-being of their subjects, and that in turn kept those subjects loyal.

After the death of Llywelyn ap Gruffudd in 1282, the heroic and royal function of poetry was greatly diminished. The poets turned to the *uchelwyr*, the remaining lesser nobility, for support as they maintained the traditional forms inherited from *Beirdd y Tywysogion*, the Poets of the Princes. The succeeding generations of *Beirdd yr Uchelwyr*, the Poets of the Nobility, continued to praise their patrons in the ancient metres of *awdl* and *englyn*, though the newly developing *cywydd deuair hirion*, or *cywydd* for short, gained the favor of the younger poets, among whom Dafydd ap Gwilym was perhaps the most influential.

Awdl

Awdl (pl. *awdlau*) is something of a blanket term that includes several varieties of poetic lines ranging from eight to nineteen syllables with a single *prifodl* or main end-rhyme throughout a number of lines and often through an entire poem. Out of approximately 150 poems that can be fairly confidently attributed to him, Dafydd composed four *awdlau* to his patrons and one satire of the poet Rhys Meigen.

Englyn

The *englyn* (pl. *englynion*) is a short epigrammatic stanza that often appears in a series. The early *englynion* had three lines each, but these gave way in the later Middle Ages to four line *englynion*. The most popular was the *englyn unodl union*, which remains so today and is the form now generally referred to simply as *englyn*. It is composed in the 'strict metres', with a single main rhyme and a complex set of rules for internal rhyme and *cynghanedd*. In addition to the *englynion* in his *awdlau* and the *englynion* in praise of the cross at Carmarthen, Dafydd composed a series of nine *englynion* that comment on each line of a Latin devotional prayer, *Anima Christi, sanctifica me* 'Spirit of Christ, sanctify me' (CDG 2), a prayer recited at the elevation of the host during Mass. Dafydd's elegy for his uncle, Llywelyn ap Gwilym, consists of thirty-five *englynion*, and he has similar series of *englynion* in praise of three other patrons. His excellence at composing, and presumably reciting, *englynion* may account for why Gruffudd Gryg calls Dafydd *bydaf englynion* 'the beehive of englynion' in *Yr Ywen uwchben Bedd Dafydd* 'The Yew Tree over Dafydd's Grave'.

Cywydd

During the early fourteenth century the *cywydd* (pl. *cywyddau*) began its rapid rise in popularity, especially as the medium for love poetry, but increasingly for praise poetry, as well. The *cywydd* is made up of any even number of seven-syllable lines forming rhyming couplets in which one of the final rhyming syllables must be stressed and the other unstressed, e.g., *cantref—nef, cêl—dawel, dig—poenedig*. *Cynghanedd* is required throughout a *cywydd*, with occasional exceptions in the first line of a couplet. The *cywydd* is an elaboration of the *traethodl*, which has seven-syllable couplets in which the rhymes do not have to be unbalanced (though two unstressed rhyming syllables never seem to occur) and there is only occasional *cynghanedd*, as in *Y Bardd a'r Brawd Llwyd* 'The Poet and the Grey Friar'.

Cynghanedd

Cynghanedd ('harmony; a singing together') is a system of patterned rhymes and matching consonants that creates a rich tapestry of sound that enhances and comments on the language with which it coexists. It is this complex of shifting effects that makes the sound of Welsh poetry at least as important as the meaning of the word. As an early proverb puts it, *Deuparth cerdd ei gwrando* 'Two thirds of a poem is listening to it.' The following notes can outline only the basic elements of the four main types of *cynghanedd: llusg, sain, croes,* and *traws.* In the examples, rhyming syllables are underlined, and matching consonants are in bold-face type.

Cynghanedd lusg: In *cynghanedd lusg,* a final syllable in the first part of a line rhymes with the stressed penultimate syllable of the line.

> Ac arfer o'th bad<u>er</u>au
>
> [*Y Bardd a'r Brawd Llwyd*, 26]

Cynghanedd sain: Cynghanedd sain forms a three-part line in which parts 1 and 2 rhyme and some or all of the consonants before the final stressed syllables of parts 2 and 3 correspond.

> Yma d<u>oeth</u> o swydd **g**<u>oeth</u> **G**aer
>
> [*Offeren y Llwyn*, 9]

Cynghanedd groes: If there is no rhyme in the line, look for matching consonants. *Cynghanedd groes* forms a two-part line with the consonants before the final stressed syllables in each part matching in the same order. Under some circumstances the consonants immediately after the final stress may be required to match.

> **M**al **h**aul y**m**y**l**au **h**oy**wl**e
>
> [*Morfudd fel yr Haul*, 21]

Cynghanedd draws: Cynghanedd draws is much like *cynghanedd groes*, but non-matching consonants intervene at the beginning of part 2.

> **Gorll**wyn ydd wyf ddyn **geirll**aes
>
> [*Morfudd fel yr Haul*, 1]

John Morris-Jones aptly summarizes the intimate, indeed inseparable, relationship between cynghanedd and meaning: [N]*i thâl y gynghanedd i draethu meddyliau wedi eu ffurfio'n barod; rhaid i'r meddyliau a draethir ynddi ymffurfio yn ei miwsig hi* 'Cynghanedd does not help to express thoughts that are already formed; thoughts that are expressed in it must form themselves in its music' (CD 82). A couple of examples from *Morfudd fel yr Haul* 'Morfudd like the Sun' might help to illustrate this:

> **Gw**iw **F**or**f**udd, **gw**ae o**f**er**f**ardd …
>
> *Excellent Morfudd! Woe to a lowly poet …*

The bold-faced consonants illustrate the balance of the two halves of the line, *Gwiw* 'excellent' vs. *gwae* 'woe', and *Forfudd* 'Morfudd' vs. *oferfardd* 'lowly poet'. Whichever of the two phrases Dafydd thought of first, the other could only be expressed once he found the proper array of consonants to match it. Or perhaps he first thought of the consonantal correspondence of *Forfudd* and *oferfardd* and constructed the line around that fortuitous coupling.

Rhyme can work in similar ways:

> Ymachl<u>udd</u> **M**orf<u>udd</u> â **m**i
>
> *Morfudd is setting from me*

Here the italicized rhymes identify Morfudd with the setting sun, while the consonantal correspondence between *Morfudd* and *mi* 'me' emphasizes both the wished for bond between her and the poet and the sorrow he feels as she departs from him, either literally or by withdrawing her favour.

Cymeriad

Another device easily visible in many poems is *cymeriad*, the linking of lines by beginning them with the same letter, word, or rhyme. The first fourteen lines of *Morfudd fel yr Haul*, for example, all begin with G-. This allows Dafydd to add emphasis to those words, and as we can see, they are words with considerable semantic heft: *Gorllwyn* 'I am waiting', *Gorlliw* 'brilliance', *Gwyl* 'See', *Goleuach* 'brighter', *Goleudaer* 'fervently bright', *Gwyr* 'She knows', etc. Even the adjective *gwiw*, frequently used in a wide range of positive senses ('apt, fit, fitting, worthy, fine, excellent, handsome, good', etc.), takes on extra weight through its repetition in this context. In lines 11 and 14, *gwiw* contrasts Morfudd's excellence or beauty with the sardonic 'excellence' of the poet's good looks as he is crying in woe. *Cymeriad* is used to quite different yet powerful effect in *Moliant Llywelyn ap Gwilym* 'Praise for Llywelyn ap Gwilym', where every line begins with *Ll-* carrying the echo of Llywelyn's name throughout the poem.

Sangiad

Sangiad 'parenthesis' allows the poet to offer commentary on what is being said, right in the middle of saying it. (In the translations in this book, the *sangiadau* are usually set apart with a dash at each end.) While frequent *sangiadau* may initially seem interruptive, they enable a poet to expand a thought or idea and often to present a new perspective or new information in a somewhat different voice, much like an aside in a play. A simple example can be found in *Galw ar Ddwynwen* 'Appealing to Dwynwen':

> Nid adwna, da ei dangnef,
> Duw a wnaeth.

> *God does not undo – good his peace –*
> *what He has done.*

As Dafydd introduced narrative into Welsh poetry, the *sangiad* not only proved to be very useful as a means of satisfying the *cynghanedd* within a line, but also offered a way to provide insight into, and commentary on, a character's thoughts and emotions as the external events of the tale or incident are being described. In *Trafferth mewn Tafarn* 'Trouble at an Inn', the *sangiadau* have yet another function as they interrupt or pause the action so that we experience the growing suspense and increasing chaos as if in slow motion, while we also hear the protagonist's growing consternation. Indeed, the *sangiadau* throughout much of this poem become a primary structural feature, raising what might otherwise be simple slapstick into a more complex humour with both visual and psychological elements that combine to create a hilarity of a sort previously unheard in Welsh verse. The *sangiadau* bring an immediacy to the poem by which we not only witness events, we are drawn into them and indeed endure them along with our poet.

One specialized form of *sangiad* is tmesis, the insertion of a word or phrase into the middle of another compound word or phrase. Dafydd uses this effectively with personal names in particular. This allows the interjection of praise, humour, or thoughtfulness while drawing attention to the poet's skill in meeting the line's metrical requirements. In *Dyddgu*, Dafydd manages to heap considerable martial praise on Dyddgu's father as he names him:

> **Ieuan**, iôr gwaywdan gwiwdad,
> **Iawnfab Gruffudd**, cythrudd cad,
> **Fab Llywelyn**, wyn wingaer,
> **Llwyd**, unben wyd, iawnben aer,

> *Ieuan – fiery-speared lord of worthy descent –*
> *true son of Gruffudd – inciter of battle –*
> *son of Llywelyn – with a white wine-fort –*
> *Llwyd, you are a chieftain, a true war leader.*

Dafydd uses the same device wryly in *Cyrchu Lleian* 'Making Advances to a Nun': *Dos i Lan falch / Llugan* 'Go to Llan-proud-Llugan'. In *Marwnad Gruffudd Gryg* 'Elegy for Gruffudd Gryg', he slips in a compliment that was surely appreciated, given that Gruffudd was still alive:

> Gruffudd, huawdl ei awdlef,
> Gryg ddoeth, myn y grog, oedd ef.
>
> *Gruffudd – eloquent his fine poetry –*
> *Gryg, he was wise, by the Cross.*

This tmetic praise takes on greater significance when we remember that Gruffudd's epithet, *cryg* 'harsh, rough, stammering' suggests a speech impediment.

Dyfalu

Another favorite device of the *cywyddwyr* is *dyfalu*. The word itself means 'to imagine', but in poetic context it refers to the piling up of numerous imaginative, even unlikely, brief comparisons or metaphors. The early *cywyddwyr* were justifiably proud of their ability to multiply such images – the more, the better. *Y Cloc* 'The Clock', Dafydd's account of a 14th-century turret clock keeping him awake, includes not only a remarkably accurate description of the machinery, it evokes visions of ducks, mills, drunken cobblers, lying tinkers, noisy dogs, scabby-bottomed saddlers, and roofers. His *Cnecian ci yn cnocian cawg* 'clattering dog banging a bowl' is familiar to dog owners even today, and the *cynghanedd*, with its repeated *cn-, c-, cn-, c-*, makes both that bowl and the ticking of the clock as audible as if we were there.

Byrfoddau a Llyfryddiaeth ✧ Abbreviations and Bibliography

APDG	Bromwich, Rachel. *Aspects of the Poetry of Dafydd ap Gwilym* (New York, 1986)
BMW	Roberts, Brynley F., ed. *Breuddwyd Maxen Wledig* (Dublin, 2005)
DGCh	Bowen, D. J. 'Dafydd ap Gwilym a Cheredigion', *Llên Cymru* 13-14 (1984), 163-209
CBT	*Cyfres Beirdd y Tywysogion*
CD	Morris-Jones, John. *Cerdd Dafod* (Rhydychen, 1925, 1959)
CDG	Johnston, Dafydd, et al. *Cerddi Dafydd ap Gwilym* (Caerdydd, 2010)
CMCS	*Cambrian* (formerly *Cambridge*) *Medieval Celtic Studies*
CT	Bollard, John K., and Anthony Griffiths. *Companion Tales to The Mabinogi* (Llandysul, 2007)
CTDG	Gruffydd, R. Geraint. 'Cywyddau Triawdaidd Dafydd ap Gwilym', YB 13, 167-77.
CWMW	Peate, Iorwerth. *Clock and Watch Makers in Wales* (Cardiff, 1960)
DG.net	http://dafyddapgwilym.net
DGIA	Edwards, Huw M. *Dafydd ap Gwilym: Influence and Analogues* (Oxford, 1996)
DGP	Bromwich, Rachel. *Dafydd ap Gwilym: Poems* (Llandysul, 1982)
EWGNP	Jacobs, Nicholas. *Early Welsh Gnomic and Nature Poetry* (London, 2012)
EWSP	Rowland, Jenny. *Early Welsh Saga Poetry* (Cambridge, 1990)
GDG	Parry, Thomas. *Gwaith Dafydd ap Gwilym* (Caerdydd, 1963)
GGG	Lewis, Barry, and Eurig Salisbury. *Gwaith Gruffudd Gryg* (Aberystwyth, 2010)
GP	Williams, G. J. ac E. J. Jones. *Gramadegau'r Penceirddiaid* (Caerdydd, 1934)
GPC	*Geiriadur Prifysgol Cymru / The University of Wales Dictionary*, online: http://welsh-dictionary.ac.uk/gpc/gpc.html
HOG	Jones, Nerys Ann. *Hywel ab Owain Gwynedd: Bardd-Dywysog* (Caerdydd, 2009)
IGP	Johnston, Dafydd. *Iolo Goch: Poems* (Llandysul, 1993)
BroDG	Jenkins, David. *Bro Dafydd ap Gwilym* (Aberystwyth, 1992)
Law	Jenkins, Dafydd. *Hywel Dda: The Law* (Llandysul, 1986)
Mab	Bollard, John K., and Anthony Griffiths. *The Mabinogi* (Llandysul, 2006)
MWM	Huws, Daniel. *Medieval Welsh Manuscripts* (Aberystwyth, 2000)
NLW	National Library of Wales / Llyfrgell Genedlaethol Cymru
PKM	Williams, Ifor. *Pedeir Keinc y Mabinogi* (Caerdydd, 1951)
PLlH	Ford, Patrick K. *The Poems of Llywarch Hen* (Berkeley, 1974)
RWM	Evans, J. Gwenogvryn. *Report on Manuscripts in the Welsh Language* (London, 1898-1910)
TA	Bollard, John K., and Anthony Griffiths. *Tales of Arthur* (Llandysul, 2010)

TYP4	Bromwich, Rachel. *Trioedd Ynys Prydein* (Cardiff, 2014)
WCD	Bartrum, Peter C. *A Welsh Classical Dictionary* (NLW, 1993)
YA	*Ystorya Adaf*, NLW Peniarth MS 7: http://www.rhyddiaithganoloesol.caerdydd.ac.uk/en/texts.php
YB	*Ysgrifau Beirniadol*

(photo courtesy of Marjorie Griffiths)

John K. Bollard is well known for his studies and translations of *The Mabinogi* and other Welsh tales. Over the years he has taught medieval Welsh prose and poetry at Harvard, Yale, the University of Massachusetts, and the University of Connecticut.

Anthony Griffiths has won the photography prize at the National Eisteddfod and produced the photographs for four volumes in collaboration with John Bollard. Their third volume, *Tales of Arthur*, was named Art/Photography Book of the Year. Anthony is also widely known as one of Wales' finest acoustic guitarists.

Other books by Bollard and Griffiths:
The Mabinogi: Legend and Landscape of Wales (2006)
Companion Tales to The Mabinogi: Legend and Landscape of Wales (2007)
Tales of Arthur: Legend and Landscape of Wales (2010)
Englynion y Beddau: Stanzas of the Graves (2015)